THE SECOND CENTURY
OF THE
ENGLISH PARLIAMENT

THE SECOND CENTURY
OF THE
ENGLISH PARLIAMENT

THE FORD LECTURES
DELIVERED IN THE
UNIVERSITY OF OXFORD
1960-1

BY

SIR GORONWY EDWARDS

CLARENDON PRESS · OXFORD
1979

46800

Oxford University Press, Walton Street, Oxford OX2 6DP

OXFORD LONDON GLASGOW
NEW YORK TORONTO MELBOURNE WELLINGTON
IBADAN NAIROBI DAR ES SALAAM CAPE TOWN
KUALA LUMPUR SINGAPORE JAKARTA HONG KONG TOKYO
DELHI BOMBAY CALCUTTA MADRAS KARACHI

British Library Cataloguing in Publication Data

Edwards, Sir, Goronwy
  The second century of the English Parliament.
  (Ford lectures).
  1. England. Parliament – History
  I. Title II. Series
  328.42'09   JN515   78–40320

  ISBN 0–19–822479–6

*Printed in Great Britain by
Richard Clay & Co Ltd., Bungay. Suffolk*

CONTENTS

EDITORIAL NOTE

SIR Goronwy Edwards (1891–1976), having studied in Oxford and Manchester and served in the Great War, was Fellow and Tutor of Jesus College, Oxford, from 1919 to 1948, Director of the Institute of Historical Research in the University of London from 1948 to his retirement in 1960, and from that year until 1964 President of the Royal Historical Society. Though primarily a historian of the Middle Ages, he was a scholar of wide interests, who in his teaching emphasized the importance of practical experience of affairs in a historian. His published work was chiefly in the field of constitutional history, English and Welsh, and so far as English institutional history is concerned, principally in the origins and early development of Parliament. While in these Ford Lectures of 1961 he made no claim to provide a general conspectus, he did aim to present some of the more significant problems that confront those who would study the subject.

Before Sir Goronwy met with the accident which led to his death in June 1976, he was intending to publish the Lectures, adding references to the sources used and other footnotes. This he did not live to do, and Lady Edwards therefore asked me to undertake the additional work and to prepare the manuscript text of the Lectures for publication. As one who owed much to her late husband's kindness, and was interested in the topic, I readily agreed. Editorially, I have taken upon myself only to make a few minor adjustments, mainly typographical and such as seemed necessary to render the spoken into the written word, to provide the references which Sir Goronwy would have added if he had been preparing the lectures for publication himself (a few of which were indicated in the manuscript), and to include an appendix. The Appendix, containing extracts in translation from the *Rotuli Parliamentorum* which illustrate points made in lectures 4 and 5, is something for which I am personally responsible. (With the *Rolls* not always easily accessible, it was thought that it might be helpful to readers.) The text of the lectures proper, save for the minor adjustments, is as Sir Goronwy left it.

I have been able to discuss some editorial points with Professor J. H. Le Patourel, and I am grateful to him for his suggestions.

J. S. ROSKELL

Parliament: its working parts and pattern of business

PARLIAMENT begins to be recorded in England under that name in the 1240s. Its second century may therefore be said to have been entered upon in the 1340s. Accordingly, our period of reference in these lectures will be the hundred years or so from about the middle of the fourteenth century onwards—a hundred years or so, not a 'nicely-calculated' hundred years.

During those hundred years or so, the number of parliaments which were held in England happens to have been also not far short of 100, about 90 to be more exact. Their duration varied, of course, but more than half of them lasted for less than six weeks, and only a minority of them had more than one session. All of them were assemblies consisting of King, Lords, and Commons. The English parliament during its first century had only occasionally included the Commons, but by the time when it reached its second century, it had become definitively a representative parliament, by which I mean a parliament which always included representatives of shires, cities, and boroughs—the representatives known collectively as 'the Commons'. By that time, too, a basic record of parliament's business had taken shape in the documents that were known as 'the rolls of the parliaments'. They are extant for all except five of the hundred or so parliaments that were held during our period. They are not by any means an exhaustive record, nor are they by any means the only record of things that were done in the parliaments: none the less they are basic and authoritative memoranda of at any rate certain kinds of important business that were consistently being transacted in parliament at that time. Their record of the business done in those parliaments will determine our line of approach, and also our attitude of mind.

We shall be considering the English parliament in its second century as 'a machine at work'. And we shall be considering the main products of the machine. At the same time, however, we shall be noticing some of the ways in which parliament's working and its products affected its place in the constitution.

From our point of view, I think that we can most usefully begin by trying to get some impression of the working parts of a parliament and the pattern of its business during the period which concerns us: and by 'pattern of business' I do not mean a catalogue of the various matters which made up the business of parliament, but the mode of transacting the business, the pattern of its transacting, whatever its various items may have been.

The addition of the Commons to the King and the Lords in parliament had not altered the basic fact that legally parliament was still, as it had always been, a single institution—King in his Council in parliament. But the addition of the representative Commons had affected the way in which the single institution—King in Council in parliament—transacted its business. Parliament still remained a single machine, but the coming of the Commons had added some new pieces to the working parts. Thus, for certain purposes, King, Council, Lords and Commons assembled together, in one and the same room. But for certain other purposes, King, Council, and Lords on the one hand, and Commons on the other, assembled apart, in separate rooms. So when parliament had come to include representatives, the holding of a parliament involved meetings which were of more than one kind. 'Yes,' you are probably saying to yourselves, 'it involved meetings of three kinds: King, Lords, and Commons all together: King and Lords by themselves: Commons by themselves. That was the scheme of things in the English parliament for centuries.' True: but was that the scheme of things in the English parliament in its second century? I think we must look at the various kinds of meetings which the holding of a parliament at that time involved. And it will help to keep things clearer if we remind ourselves that those various kinds of meetings can be distinguished topographically as well as in other ways. For when parliaments met at Westminster— and out of the hundred or so parliaments of our period, there were only about a dozen that did not meet at Westminster—most of the various kinds of meetings which the holding of those parliaments involved had established places of assembly, each in a definite room. (1) There was one meeting which in several ways stood apart from all the rest. This was the initial assembling of the parliament. For this meeting, the King and all the Lords and all the Commons assembled together in one room. The room which they used for this initial assembling was the room in the royal palace of Westminster known as the Painted Chamber, so called because it was decorated with mural paintings. One of the ways in which this initial meeting stood apart from all the rest was this. Except for certain legal formalities, the business at this first meeting of the parliament consisted of a single item: to hear a statement made by some royal minister, or other worshipful personage, on the King's behalf. The purport of the statement is indicated by the fact that it was usually referred to as 'the causes of summons' or sometimes as 'the points of the parliament'. It stated the business which the King required parliament to consider, and quite frequently it actually formulated various questions to which the King asked for specific answers—among the commonest of these being the question what taxation the Lords and the Commons were willing to grant to him. From the circumstance that specific answers to specific questions were often required, the statement setting out 'the points of the parliament' was often called compendiously 'the charge'. Having thus set out the King's business that had to be treated, the statement then went on to announce the King's willingness to receive and answer petitions for the redress of grievances suffered by his subjects whether individually or in common, and a date during the succeeding week or so was usually specified for the handing in of such petitions.

It was therefore in these initial meetings of each parliament that the pattern of parliamentary business was set. The pattern was set in two ways: firstly by specifying the 'points'; and secondly by inviting the petitions. The 'points' required answers from Lords and Commons; I repeat—answers from Lords and Commons, from the Commons as well as the Lords. The idea that the Commons came to parliament merely as petitioners is a delusion: they came also as answerers, and while they were invited to petition if they wished, they were required to answer whether they wished to answer or not. The petitions required answers from the King. Finding and formulating those various answers—such was the general pattern and purport of parliament's business. Of course, the finding and formulating of these answers was often not at all a simple matter and sometimes became a lengthy process: but basically that is what they were doing—finding and formulating answers of one sort or another to 'the points' on the one hand, and to the petitions on the other.

When once the initial assembly of parliament had occurred, King, Lords, and Commons did not again meet together in the Painted Chamber during the remainder of that particular parliament. From time to time during the remainder of the particular parliament, King, Lords, and Commons certainly *did* meet together in a single room. But the single room that they used for those subsequent meetings was not the Painted Chamber. So we have registered our first variety of parliamentary meeting—the initial assembling in the Painted Chamber.

It is of course common knowledge that after the initial assembling of the whole parliament, the Lords and the Commons spent most of their time working apart in two separate rooms. That gives us our second and third variety of parliamentary meeting.

(2) The room that was used by the Lords as their separate meeting-place was invariably the room in the palace of Westminster known at first as the White Chamber, but later called the Parliament Chamber. The Lords continued to use that same room down to 1801.

(3) The room that was used by the Commons is not so easily determined. Now of course it is not a matter of great importance to determine exactly which room the Commons used. The basically important point is that they used a room which was distinct from and separated from the room used by the Lords. But for anyone with any historical sense, the location of the room which was the meeting-place of the Commons of medieval England must be a matter of considerable interest. So I make no apology for touching on the point, particularly as the books seem

to me to be both more unanimous and more categorical about the matter than they have any real right to be.

The traditional view is pretty sweeping, that the habitual meeting-place of the Commons in medieval parliaments was the Chapter House of Westminster Abbey. That traditional view, however, seems to be based almost entirely on one word in the parliament roll of 1376. One of the entries in that roll records that the Commons were told to withdraw after the initial assembling of parliament to 'leur ancienne place' in the Chapter House.[1] And that statement is copied verbatim in the corresponding entry in the roll for the succeeding parliament of January 1377.[2] Most English writers have translated the phrase 'leur ancienne place' as 'their ancient place': but the French word 'ancienne', then as now, meant 'ancient' not only in the sense of 'a long time ago', but also in the sense of 'former', a *former* time not necessarily long ago. The phrase 'leur ancienne place' must therefore be interpreted in the context of the evidence as a whole. That evidence in this case presents a teasing jig-saw, but a few things at least are clear. The Chapter House is specifically recorded in the parliament rolls as the Commons' meeting-place on some six occasions, the earliest in 1352 and the latest in 1395.[3] Nine years earlier, however, than 1352, in 1343, the parliament roll records the Commons as meeting in the Painted Chamber.[4] Moreover, they are recorded as still meeting in the Painted Chamber by the rolls of the parliaments of 1365, 1366, and 1373.[5] It is also necessary to notice that the parliament roll of 1352, in which the Commons' use of the Chapter House is first specifically recorded, happens also to mention that the Commons on that occasion held their first separate meeting in the Painted Chamber, but then moved into the Chapter House because the Painted Chamber was required for another meeting.[6] So there can be no doubt, at any rate, that the Commons were meeting in the Painted Chamber on five occasions between

[1] *Rotuli Parliamentorum*, ed. J. Strachey (London, 1767-83), ii.322(8).

[2] Ibid. 363(18).

[3] Ibid. 237(8), 322(8) (1376), 363(18) (Jan. 1377); iii.5(11) (Oct. 1377), 185(10) (Nov. 1384), 329(1) (1395).

[4] Ibid. ii.136(8).   [5] Ibid. 283(7), 289(7), 316(4).   [6] Ibid. 237(8).

1343 and 1373, and that on one of those occasions, in 1352, they began by using the Painted Chamber, and then went to the Chapter House because the Painted Chamber was wanted for some other meeting: in other words, in 1352, at any rate, the Commons used the Chapter House as an alternative to the Painted Chamber. The parliament rolls also show that the Painted Chamber would be a *convenient* room for the Commons to use. The rolls of 1365 and 1366 expressly say that when the initial assembly of the whole parliament in the Painted Chamber was at an end, the King took with him the prelates, dukes, earls, and barons into the White Chamber, and the Commons of shires, cities, and boroughs remained in the Painted Chamber.[7] So the change-over after the initial meeting could be made with the minimum of bother: the Commons, who were by far the most numerous section of parliament, could just stay where they were. The evidence as it stands, therefore, indicates pretty clearly that the Painted Chamber was used by the Commons as their meeting-room earlier than the Chapter House, and that in the first instance the Chapter House was assigned to them as a substitute when the Painted Chamber was not available. One such occasion is definitely recorded in 1352, and the reason which operated in 1352—that the Painted Chamber was wanted for another meeting—would be liable to recur. By 1376, therefore, it would be quite possible for the Clerk of the Parliament to describe the Chapter House as the 'ancienne place' of the Commons—it *would* be their 'former place', in the sense that it would be a place that they had used before: they had used it, to our knowledge, in 1352; and equally to our knowledge, they had *not* used it in 1343, 1365, 1366, and 1373.

The meeting-place of the Commons which is last recorded in the parliament rolls is the *Refectory* of Westminster Abbey. Oddly enough, the earliest specific reference to the Refectory and the latest specific reference to the Chapter House come together; the parliament roll records that in the initial meeting of the parliament of January 1395, the Commons were instructed that they would meet on the morrow 'either in the Chapter House or in the

Refectory of Westminster'.[8] It may seem to us very odd that the room which the Commons were to use should have been still undecided so late as the day preceding the very day of their meeting, but such is the record in the parliament roll. And unluckily the roll does not tell us which of the two rooms the Commons eventually did use on that occasion. But at any rate there is no specific record in the parliament rolls subsequent to 1395 that the Commons ever used the Chapter House again. And starting with the very next parliament of January 1397 there are specific records that the Commons did use the Refectory in five of the parliaments between 1397 and 1416.[9] Where they met after 1416 the parliament rolls do not specify. But it is at least clear that over the two decades between 1397 and 1416, the Commons seem to have been meeting in the Refectory of Westminster rather than in the Chapter House. What caused the change is not clear, but it may well have been made because for some reason it had become more convenient for the monks that the Commons should meet in the Refectory rather than in the Chapter House. Anyway, the substantive point is that the Chapter House of Westminster has no assured claim to be regarded as the earliest meeting-place, or as the habitual meeting-place, or as the latest meeting-place of the Commons in medieval parliaments. So far as evidence goes, the Chapter House was one of three meeting-rooms which the Commons used at different times during the fourteenth and fifteenth centuries. But the Chapter House does of course have for us the unique interest of being the only one of the three that has survived to our own day. The Painted Chamber was destroyed in the fire of 1834. The Refectory of the Abbey was dismantled at the Dissolution, and only portions of its walls now remain.

I have already said that one of the two main functions of parliament during our period was to make answers to the 'points' raised on the King's behalf in the opening 'charge'. Some of those answers—the answers, for instance, to royal requests for taxation—concerned the Lords as well as the Commons, and it was therefore

---

[8] Ibid. iii.329(1).

[9] Ibid. 338(8) (Jan. 1397), 523(9) (Jan. 1404); iv.34(5) (Nov. 1414), 70(4) (Mar. 1416), 94(3) (Oct. 1416).

necessary that Lords and Commons should consult together before the answers were made. There are clear signs in the parliament rolls by the beginning of our period that such consultations were already taking place, and as the fourteenth century goes on, there are repeated references to those consultations in the parliament rolls.[10] In the rolls, the consultations are usually described by the French word 'entrecommuner'—to consult together, to confer, to intercommune. The most convenient word for us to use is the word 'conference', provided always we bear in mind that these medieval conferences or intercommunings between Lords and Commons were, in their scope and purpose, quite unlike the Conference of Both Houses between the House of Lords and the House of Commons in later times. This medieval 'conference' was therefore yet another variety—a fourth variety—of meeting which the medieval parliament involved. How did this medieval 'conference' of Lords and Commons work during our period?

(4) That the conference of Lords and Commons was an important piece among the working parts of parliament in our period is indicated by the circumstances in which the parliament rolls come to give us their earliest description of it. In the parliament of January 1352, the statement of the 'causes of summons' was made by Sir William Shareshull, Chief Justice of the King's Bench, and it contained one item that was unusual. He was making his statement on Tuesday 17 January.[11] After setting out the 'points' of the parliament, he told the Commons to think them over until the next day, Wednesday 18 January, and then to assemble on that Wednesday morning, immediately after sunrise (8.00 a.m.) in the Painted Chamber, to discuss those 'points'. So far this was along the usual lines. But then Shareshull added some further instructions that so far as we know were not usual. In order, he said, that the business of parliament should be carried through expeditiously, the Commons were to get together before leaving Westminster that very day (Tuesday 17 January), and choose twenty-four or

---

[10] These 'consultations' are more fully dealt with in the author's Creighton Lecture in History for 1957, *The Commons in Medieval English Parliaments* (London, 1958), pp. 5-25, 28-36.

[11] *Rot. Parl.* ii.237(6,7).

thirty from among themselves: those twenty-four or thirty, on the next day (Wednesday 18 January) were to confer with a number of the Lords whom the King would send to meet them in the Painted Chamber.[12] The rest of the Commons, Shareshull explained, would withdraw from the Painted Chamber—that is, after holding their sunrise meeting in that room—and would go to the Chapter House of the Abbey.[13] Thereby, as you can see, the Painted Chamber would be left free for the conference. (You will remember that I said a moment ago that the Commons went to the Chapter House in 1352 because the Painted Chamber was wanted for another meeting. That other meeting was the conference of Lords and Commons.) Shareshull went on to say that when the 'twenty-four or thirty' of the Commons had conferred with the lords in the Painted Chamber, they were to join the general body of their companions in the Chapter House, and report to them what had been said in the conference. There would then (he said) be a discussion 'among all the Commons' until they reached what he called a 'common accord'. When such an 'accord' had been reached, the twenty-four or thirty were to report to the King what the general body of the Commons had thus 'accorded'.[14] The parliament roll of 1352 subsequently shows that the procedure which Shareshull had laid down was duly followed. What is the implication of his speech? It presumably implies that conferences between Lords and Commons had not been working as expeditiously as they might have done, and that the government was trying to improve the conference procedure by removing or lessening the occasions of delay. In other words, the conferences of Lords and Commons were sufficiently important in the working of parliament to become in 1352 a matter for what we would call 'government intervention'.

These conferences, on the general lines of what might be called the 1352 model, continue to be recorded as a normal feature of English parliamentary procedure not only in the latter years of Edward III, but also in the reigns of Richard II and Henry IV. In the years subsequent to 1352, some details of their working were evidently modified by usage. Thus by 1373 it had become the

<hr>

[12] Ibid. 237(8).   [13] Ibid.   [14] Ibid.

custom that the names of the Lords' delegates to the conferences were suggested by the Commons,[15] though both Richard II and Henry IV made a formal protestation that the King could nominate any lords that he wished:[16] in practice, however, the names suggested by the Commons seem always to have been accepted. Most commonly the Commons asked for some such number of the Lords as nine[17] or twelve,[18] often drawn equally from the three grades of bishops, earls, and barons. In the 1370s, too, the number of the Commons' delegates is stated in one of the parliament rolls to be 'some such' 'small and reasonable' number as six or ten:[19] the very words of the statement sufficiently indicate that the number of the Commons' delegates was not rigidly fixed—it probably varied from time to time, as we know that the number of the Lords' delegates certainly did. Another development was that by the 1370s the Commons were not only allowed in effect to nominate the lords who attended the conference, but were also left to take the initiative in asking for the conference, and usually they put forward their request quite early in the session: it is noticeable, however, that they did not ask for the conference until after they had had at least two or three days' discussion among themselves,[20] and on some occasions not until after still longer discussion than two or three days.[21] It also becomes very clear in the parliament rolls of the 1370s and 1380s that these conferences might be elaborate and prolonged: both lots of delegates used to report back to their respective main bodies as often as they thought fit, and evidently did so until the conference eventually reached an agreed view on the matters before it—and of those matters, the commonest would appear to have been taxation. So the conference might involve not a single meeting, but a series of meetings, between the two delegations: in fact, the parliament roll of 1373,

[15] Ibid. 316(5).

[16] Ibid. iii.145(8) (Feb. 1382), 486(10) (1402).

[17] Ibid. 145(8) (Feb. 1383), 167(9) (Apr. 1384).

[18] Ibid. ii.322(8) (1376), 363(18) (Jan. 1377); iii.486(11) (1402).

[19] Ibid. iii.36(23).

[20] As in February 1383 (ibid. 145(8)).

[21] In 1407 the Commons did not request an inter-communing with the Lords until the session was three weeks old (ibid. 610(18)).

for example, states explicitly that the conference went on during six days.[22] Taken together, therefore, the evidence indicates that the conferences of Lords and Commons during our period played a much more formative part in the work of parliament than did the Conferences of Both Houses in later centuries.

The rooms in which these fourteenth-century conferences were held are hardly ever specifically named. We have seen that in the parliament of 1352 the conference of Lords and Commons was to be held in the Painted Chamber, and that it was in order to free the Painted Chamber for the conference that the general body of the Commons were moved on that occasion from the Painted Chamber to the Chapter House. In the parliament of 1373, however, the parliament roll happens to mention that the conference of Lords and Commons on that occasion took place in a room of the palace known as the Chamberlain's Chamber.[23] The roll also happens to mention that the Commons of that parliament held their separate meetings in the Painted Chamber.[24] Now the Chamberlain's Chamber was one of the normal meeting-places of the parliamentary Triers of Petitions, so that it would not always be free for conferences. We may, therefore, reasonably surmise that conferences of Lords and Commons met in the Chamberlain's Chamber when it was available, but if the Chamberlain's Chamber was not free, then the conferences of Lords and Commons would meet in the Painted Chamber. In that case, the Painted Chamber would be made available for the conference by moving the general body of the Commons into the Chapter House over the way. That at least is what actually happened in 1352. The transfer of the Commons from a meeting-room within the Palace of Westminster to the less congruous meeting-place in the Chapter House of the Abbey is a puzzling development. Why did it happen? Well, the need of using the Painted Chamber for the conferences of Lords and Commons is a consideration that helps to explain it.

We have now noted four varieties of meeting which the holding of a parliament involved during our period—the initial meeting of King, Lords, and Commons all together; the separate

---

[22] *Rot. Parl.* ii.316(5).   [23] Ibid.   [24] Ibid. (1), (4).

meetings of the Lords; the separate meetings of the Commons; and the conferences of Lords and Commons.

(5) One more variety completes the catalogue. Variety No. 5 is the meetings of King, Lords, and Commons which took place in the White Chamber, that is, in the room which for the greater part of the time was used by the Lords as their separate meeting-place. For these meetings, the Commons joined the King and the Lords in the White Chamber; they did so as many times during the course of a parliament as the transaction of business required; and in some parliaments these meetings were evidently pretty numerous. There is one point about them which concerns us for our purpose.

When we say that 'the Commons joined the King and the Lords in the White Chamber', what do we mean by 'the Commons'? When King, Lords, and Commons assembled together for the initial meeting of the parliament in the Painted Chamber, all the Commons—or, at any rate, all who had arrived—attended the meeting. Are we to suppose that all the Commons joined the King and the Lords in the White Chamber? So far as I can make out, it has been silently assumed that they did. I don't mean, of course, that it has been assumed that every man Jack actually went. But it has, I think, been silently assumed that every man Jack of the Commons could go if he wanted to. That assumption, I think, needs to be questioned, scrutinized.

Take, for instance, the parliament of November 1373. We have already seen that the Commons had the duty, among other things, of answering the 'points' that had been raised in the opening 'charge' delivered in the initial meeting of the parliament. Now in the 1370s, their first step in making an answer was to request a conference of Lords and Commons. In the parliament of 1373 they appeared in the White Chamber to make this request on 23 November.[25] 'On which day', says the Clerk of the Parliament in the parliament roll, 'there came into the White Chamber some of the Commons in the name of all (*aucuns des Communes en nom de tous*) and requested . . . [a conference]'. 'Some of the Commons

---

[25] Ibid. (5).

in the name of all.' 'Some . . . in the name of all.' That would be the ordinary way of describing a delegation, a chosen number acting on behalf of a larger body: something much more specific than a chance number of the larger body just happening to turn up on the particular occasion. Anyway, not 'all': only 'some'. Some in the name of all. That was the position in the parliament of 1373.

The very next parliament, in April 1376, happened to be the famous parliament called, then and afterwards, the Good Parliament. By a piece of good fortune there is a very illuminating account of some of the proceedings of the Good Parliament in a chronicle published by V. H. Galbraith in 1927 under the title *The Anonimalle Chronicle 1333–1381* of St. Mary's Abbey, York. There are clear signs that the account of the parliament of 1376[26] was derived from an eye-witness, and there is general agreement that the chronicle provides a very valuable complement to the record of the 1376 parliament in the parliament roll. The chronicler describes several of the occasions during the session when the Commons, as he expresses it, 'went into parliament into the presence of the Lords in the White Chamber'. On the first of these occasions the chronicler emphasizes that the Commons decided among themselves that they would (as he puts it) 'all go together in a serried body before the Lords'.[27] (The fact that they 'decided' to do this surely suggests in itself that it was unusual.) But when they arrived at what he calls 'the door of parliament'—that is, the door of the White Chamber—only some of them were allowed to enter, and the rest were shut out. Their spokesman, Sir Peter de la Mare, a knight of the shire for Hereford, protested against the exclusion of those who had been shut out, and declared that he would not deliver his message until they had all been admitted. As the King was absent from parliament through illness, the Duke of Lancaster was acting as his lieutenant, and he said: 'Sir Piers, there is no need for so many of the Commons to come in for the purpose of giving an answer [note the phrase], but twelve or thirteen

---

[26] *The Anonimalle Chronicle 1333–1381*, ed. V. H. Galbraith (Manchester, 1927), pp. 79–94.

[27] Ibid., p. 83.

will be enough at one time, *as has been usual hitherto*'.[28] Sir Piers, however, insisted, and in the end he had his way, whereupon he delivered his message: this was a request for a conference of Lords and Commons, which (as I have said) was at that period the Commons' opening gambit in the process of making their answer. Now we know that there was a great deal of discontent in 1376, and it is obvious that the Commons were staging a demonstration, but for our present purpose the interest of the incident lies in what the Duke of Lancaster said, and particularly in his remark that the existing practice was for the Commons to go to the King and the Lords in the White Chamber, not as a whole body, but 'twelve or thirteen at any one time'—in other words, not *all* the Commons, but only a delegation of them. Now Lancaster in 1376 was not yet '*Old* John of Gaunt, *time-honour'd* Lancaster', but a man of his position and experience might be presumed to know something about such matters as these. Fortunately we need not rely upon mere presumption: for what he says agrees perfectly with what is recorded in the parliament roll for the immediately preceding parliament of 1373: we have already seen that in the parliament of 1373 the Commons' request for a conference was made by 'some of the Commons in the name of all', i.e. by a delegation. So the anonymous chronicler of 1376 had good reason for emphasizing that the Commons '*decided* among themselves that they would *all go together in a serried body* before the Lords'. For evidently it was an unusual decision. But then the occasion was unusual, and the Commons were staging a demonstration by departing from usage. If 1376 had been a more normal occasion, they would presumably have taken the normal course of choosing a delegation to appear before the Lords 'in the name of all', as they had done in the preceding parliament of 1373.

We have now come across this mechanism of delegation in two distinct contexts in connection with the Commons in parliament during at any rate the earlier part of our period: on the one hand they sent a delegation to the conference of Lords and Commons; and on the other hand they sent a delegation to give 'answers' to

[28] Ibid., p. 84.

the King and the Lords in the White Chamber. Most unluckily, there seems to be no record of the names of those who served on any of these Commons' delegations. But two things about them may be noticed. We have seen that when Sir William Shareshull instructed the Commons about their conference with the Lords in 1352,[29] he told them that the twenty-four or thirty delegates whom they were to choose were to do three things: firstly, attend the conference with the Lords (having already, of course, attended the sunrise meeting of the Commons); secondly, report what had happened at the conference to the general body of the Commons; and thirdly, after the general body of the Commons had reached a common accord, the twenty-four or thirty were to report to the King and the Lords what the general body of the Commons had decided. In other words, according to the 1352 instructions, the delegation of the Commons, who went to the White Chamber for the purpose of giving 'answers', were intended to be the same delegation as served in the conference of Lords and Commons. Whether that intention was always literally carried out we cannot say, but perhaps we may reasonably surmise that, in any one parliament, the Commons' delegates to the King and the Lords and their delegates to the conference of Lords and Commons would be largely, if not entirely, the same persons. That is the first thing to be noticed. The second is this. There are some scattered pieces of circumstantial evidence which suggest that the Commons' delegations to the King and the Lords were drawn, not from the Commons in general, but only from among the knights of the shires. Thus in the parliament of 1362 one of the 'points' of the 'charge' was the question whether Calais should be set up as a staple town.[30] The Lords answered in favour of the idea. The Commons answered that they had spoken to a number of merchants about it, and some had said that it would be a good thing, while others had said the contrary, so the Commons suggested that the merchants should be consulted direct, which seems to have been done at the close of the session. Now this answer is recorded in the parliament roll of 1362 as having been given by

[29] *Rot. Parl.* ii.237(8).   [30] Ibid. 268(1).

what are called 'the knights of the shires'.[31] This seems to indicate that in 1362 at any rate the Commons' 'answers' were made to the King and Lords by delegates who were all knights of the shires. And on some other occasions, too, there are further pieces of circumstantial evidence which seem to point in the same direction.

Having cast an eye over the main working parts of the parliamentary machine during our period and also—for greater clarity, I hope—over the actual rooms in which each of those working parts functioned, we can now proceed to consider the main products of the machine, and that is what I shall be trying to do in the rest of these lectures. Its main products were two in number. On the one hand, taxation. On the other hand, petitions and bills. I propose to consider them in that order: firstly taxation, secondly petitions and bills.

There is a reason for giving priority to taxation which is more substantial than the formal one of taking one's cue from the sequence of entries in the parliament rolls. It has been said, by G. O. Sayles, that 'out of the twenty-one parliaments which met in the first ten years of Edward III's reign, only five voted supplies.'[32] Now the first ten years of Edward III's reign were the years 1327–37, so they are on the very threshold of the period with which we are concerned. It is true to say that out of the hundred or so parliaments that met during the hundred years or so of our period, only some eighteen did *not* vote supplies. In other words, the incidence of taxation in the business of parliament was completely reversed after the first ten years of Edward III. So even if it were granted that 'fiscal measures' 'came up for discussion far too intermittently and irregularly to give them [the Commons in parliament] a sense of coherence and integration', that would not be true after 1337: in our period what were 'intermittent and irregular' were the parliaments in which fiscal measures did *not* come up for discussion. So presumably—even as Sayles premises—one must suppose that fiscal measures *did* have some very substantial effect in promoting the coherence and integration of the Commons.

---

[31] Ibid. 269(7).
[32] G. O. Sayles, *The Medieval Foundations of England* (2nd edn., 1950), p. 460.

Taxation I

I SAID last time that the two main products of the parliamentary machine which we would be considering would be (1) Taxation and (2) Petitions and Bills, and that I would take Taxation first. I take Taxation before Petitions and Bills partly because that is the order in which the parliament rolls record them. I should explain in passing that the parliament rolls of our period conform pretty closely to a standard pattern. They always begin with a record of the initial assembling of the parliament, including a summary, sometimes longer and sometimes shorter, of the 'points' of the 'charge'. They almost always end with a section which is usually headed 'Petitions of the Commons' or 'Common Petitions', and this section quite often occupies more space than all the rest of the roll put together. In-between those first and last sections the clerk enters all the rest of the business that he records, in no fixed order, but quite frequently he enters the grant of taxation immediately after his record of the initial meeting of the parliament. In any case, the grants of taxation are entered before the 'Petitions of the Commons'. But there is yet another reason for giving priority to Taxation in our present discussion. The second century of the English parliament happened to coincide almost exactly with the period of the Hundred Years War. That war created for the English government financial problems which immediately made themselves felt in the business of parliament. During the first ten years of Edward III's reign, i.e. from 1327 to 1337, and therefore before the Hundred Years War got really under way, out of some twenty parliaments which met in those ten years, only five made grants of taxation.[1] During the last forty years of Edward III's

[1] The parliaments of 1327, 1332 (Sept.), 1334 (Sept.), 1336, and 1337.

reign, i.e. from 1337 to 1377, out of some thirty parliaments
which met, only five did *not* make grants of taxation.[2] During the
hundred years or so which concern us, out of some ninety
parliaments which met, only some eighteen did not make grants
of taxation. It is therefore clear that of the various 'points' to
which the King demanded 'answers' from his parliaments, there
was during our period no 'point' which recurred so frequently or
so steadily—repeat, no 'point' which recurred so frequently or so
steadily—as taxation.

Now in one sense, the story of this parliamentary taxation is
very familiar. Stubbs gave a good deal of attention to it, and in his
Constitutional History he worked out the sequence of the grants of
taxation made by the parliaments of the fourteenth and fifteenth
centuries. His account of those grants was a characteristic and
remarkable piece of pioneer work, and it is still valuable. But it
was of necessity embedded mainly in the *narrative* chapters of his
Constitutional History, and it therefore had to be rather chrono-
logical in treatment. His account of parliamentary taxation would
have gained in interest if the scale of the *Constitutional History* had
allowed him to do two divergent but complementary things: on
the one hand, to stand further away from the *sequence* of the grants
in order to see more of its *pattern*; and on the other hand, to stand
quite close to it at some points in order to see more of its detail;
for, after all, these grants were documents of great precision, and
some of them become more significant when viewed at closer
range.

Taxation, then as now, was broadly of two kinds: direct, and
indirect. Parliaments in our period granted both kinds, sometimes
separately, often together. But it makes for clarity if we consider
them separately.

It will be convenient if we take Indirect Taxation first. During
our period this was mainly in the form of duties on exports and
imports, especially upon exports, and particularly upon wool,
which was England's main product for the export market. For our
purposes, there were two duties which were specially important.

---

[2] The parliaments of 1354, 1361, 1363, 1366, and 1376.

On the one hand, there was the tax known as the 'subsidy on wool, woolfells and hides' (which for short we will call the 'subsidy on wool' or the 'wool-subsidy'): this was an export duty. On the other hand, there was the tax known as tonnage and poundage: tonnage was an import duty on wine, and poundage was broadly speaking an import duty on commodities other than wine, and an export duty on commodities other than wool, woolfells and hides.

Now the subsidy on wool and the tonnage and poundage were not only very productive forms of taxation for the King: they also happen to be of quite considerable constitutional interest in connection with the English parliament during its second century. By then, there was pretty general agreement in England that taxation, whether direct or indirect, should not be taken arbitrarily, but only with some sort of consent. By the beginning of our period it was established usage that the consent required for *direct* taxation was the consent of parliament. But the consent required for indirect taxes, like the subsidy on wool and tonnage and poundage, was not so clear. Such taxes were actually paid at the ports by the merchants who handled the trade, and at first the consent of the merchants to these taxes was regarded, at any rate by the King, as sufficient. Indirect taxation, however, was apt, then as now, to be passed on by the merchants to the producers or consumers of the commodities that were taxed, and the cry was soon raised among the King's subjects that in the granting of *indirect* taxation the consent of the merchants was not enough, but that the consent ought to be that of parliament, in which the representatives spoke for the whole community, upon whom the indirect taxes would ultimately fall. When, therefore, we find parliaments in the course of the fourteenth century demanding that taxation ought to be granted by consent of parliament, what they had particularly in mind was not taxation in general, but indirect taxation, and when they said 'granted by consent of parliament', they were thinking of the consent of parliament in contradistinction to the consent of the merchants, not in contradistinction to arbitrary taxation with no consent by anybody.

We can conveniently take up the story of parliamentary grants

of indirect taxation at 1351. Here is one of those cases in which a
close-up of some of the details is necessary. In the parliament of
1351, a petition was made in the name of what is called 'la Commune' ('the community') against the subsidy of 40s. on the sack of
wool which, the petition says, 'the merchants have granted to our
lord the King'.³ The petition asks that 'any such grant made outside parliament' should be treated as null. But it then goes on to
say something more. 'In case', it says, 'it is the King's pleasure, in
this his great necessity, to have the aforesaid 40s. for a half year or a
year, [the 'Commune' asks that] he may be pleased to show his
will to the peers and 'commune' of the land, for their comfort.' In
other words, parliament was prepared to listen to a request from
the King for a grant of the subsidy on wool, provided he could
show that he was in real necessity. But the grant must be made by
'the peers and community of the land', i.e. by parliament and not
by the merchants, and it must be for half a year or a year, i.e. for a
period that was both definite and short. The parliament roll goes
on to record that, after this petition, 'the King showed to the
Lords and Commons assembled in parliament that his great
necessity still continues . . . and the Lords and Commons by common assent granted him the said subsidy for two years' from the
ensuing Michaelmas—i.e. from Michaelmas 1351 to Michaelmas
1353.⁴ (So when in the petition they had said 'half a year or a
year', they evidently did not intend their words to be taken
absolutely literally.) Now that grant of the subsidy on wool by the
parliament of 1351 proved to be a turning point, and the manner
of it proved to be symptomatic too: from 1351 onwards, parliamentary grants of indirect taxes in the form of the subsidy on wool
are a recurring item in the parliament rolls. All this is pretty
familiar. But what exactly is meant by saying that from 1351
onwards these parliamentary grants of the wool-subsidy were a
recurring item? In what sense, or senses, did they 'recur'?

(i) What was the duration of these parliamentary grants of the
wool subsidy? I have already said that the parliament of 1351
granted the subsidy for a period of two years. How about sub-

---

³ *Rot. Parl.* ii.229(22).   ⁴ Ibid.

sequent grants? Well, the next was for three years, the next after that was for six years, the next after that again was for three years.[5] After that, for the rest of Edward III's reign, the grants were all for periods of either two or three years.[6] Or again in the reign of Henry IV, the grants were mostly for either two or three years,[7] though there were two grants to Henry IV for only one year at a time.[8] A grant for as long a period as six years, such as was made on one occasion to Edward III, was unusual. It is now necessary to ask another question.

(ii) What sort of a sequence did these recurring grants of the wool subsidy form? Did they form a broken sequence, or did they dovetail into one another, so as to produce a sequence that was chronologically unbroken? The answer is that they were in fact so dovetailed that they did form an uninterrupted sequence. Thus the grant of 1351 (as we have seen) was for two years from Michaelmas 1351 to Michaelmas 1353; the next was for three years from Michaelmas 1353 to Michaelmas 1356, and so on for the rest of Edward III's reign. Or again in Henry IV's reign, the first grant was for three years from Michaelmas 1399 to Michaelmas 1402; the next for three years from Michaelmas 1402 to Michaelmas 1405, and so on. During the reign of Richard II, in the 1380s there were a few short 'interruptions' (as they are called in the parliament rolls) between some of the grants, but these were short and at least two of them[9] are recorded to have been deliberately made by parliament in order to emphasize the principle that the parliamentary grant of the wool subsidy 'proceeds' (as they put it) 'from the free and spontaneous grant of Lords and Commons, [and] may not be claimed as of right and custom'. But the majority of the grants of the wool subsidy under Richard II, as under Edward III (after 1351) and Henry IV, dovetailed into one another so as to form an absolutely continuous sequence. The

---

[5] Made in 1353, 1355, and 1362, respectively (ibid. 252(33), 265(11), 273(35)).

[6] Made in 1365 for 3 years, in 1368 for 2, in 1369 for 3, in 1372 for 2, in 1373 for 2, and in 1376 for 3 (ibid. 285(9), 295(9), 300(10), 310(10), 317(12), 322(9)).

[7] In 1399 for 3 years, in 1402 for 3, in 1404 (Oct.) for 2, in 1407 for 2, and in 1410 for 2 (ibid. iii.425(65), 493(28), 546(9), 612(26), 635(45)).

[8] In 1406 for 1 year, in 1411 for 1 (ibid. 568(9), 648(10)).

[9] Ibid. iii.104(40) (1381), 204(11) (1385).

practical importance of that general fact will be underlined if we now ask yet another question.

(iii) How was the making of such a grant timed in relation to the expiry of the preceding grant? It is clear that the great majority of these subsidies on wool were in practice authorized by parliament before the expiry of the preceding grant, usually some months before. Thus, a subsidy was granted in April 1379,[10] six months before the current subsidy was due to run out; or again in December 1407,[11] nine months before the current subsidy ran out at Michaelmas 1408. The few exceptions to this practice were due to the accident that parliament was not called to meet in sufficient time before the expiry-date of the current grant.

(iv) The last point to notice about the subsidies on wool concerns the rates at which they were granted. These rates often varied from one grant to another. In the grants, the rate of the subsidy was defined at so many shillings on the sack of wool (i.e. shorn wool), so many shillings on a specified number of woolfells (i.e. the sheepskins with the wool attached), and so many shillings on an amount of hides known as the 'last'. Each of those rates was varied at different times; moreover in the 1370s parliament began to impose higher rates on foreign merchants than on English merchants, which made the number of variables still greater. Just as an example, I will indicate the *range* of the variations in the rate imposed on the sack of wool. In the grant of 1351, which we have taken as our starting point, parliament granted 40s. on the sack, which had been the rate previously granted by the merchants. During the rest of our period the highest rate granted was 43s. 4d., and down to the end of Henry V's reign, 43s. 4d. was the rate prescribed in the great majority of the grants. Lower rates were sometimes prescribed, the lowest being 20s. on the sack, but only in a few grants was the rate put lower than 40s. and none of those rates below 40s. were in force for any length of time, at any rate until the succession of Henry VI in 1422. After 1422, the rate per sack of wool for English merchants was 33s. 4d. It is therefore evident that, on the whole, parliament did not use its power of

---

[10] Ibid. 57(13).   [11] Ibid. 612(26).

assenting to the subsidy as a means of forcing down the rates at which the subsidy was granted.

The other main form of indirect taxation that concerns us—tonnage and poundage—can be dealt with quite briefly, as its history, from our point of view, is largely a repetition of the history of the wool subsidy. It was at first granted by the consent of the merchants, but from the 1380s onwards tonnage and poundage becomes the subject of parliamentary grants, which recur in much the same way as the subsidy on wool—in fact, tonnage and poundage was quite often granted by parliament at the same times, and for the same periods, as the wool subsidy.

We have now seen that these parliamentary grants of indirect taxation, as they actually developed in practice, gave to English kings after 1351 an established source of revenue which they had not possessed in an established form before that date. These indirect taxes needed only to be granted permanently to become a standing addition to the King's standing revenue—'his own', as they called it. And that further development in fact duly occurred. In 1398, the subsidy on wool was granted to Richard II for life.[12] In 1415 not only the subsidy on wool but also tonnage and poundage were granted for life to Henry V.[13] In 1453 again all three were granted to Henry VI for life,[14] and thereafter to his successors in time down to James I.[15] I am not forgetting, of course, that the life-grant to Richard II is usually interpreted against the background of his projected 'tyranny'—or whatever is the right word—and that the life-grant to Henry V is interpreted against the shining background of St. Crispin's Day, and as a tribute to the conquering hero of Agincourt. But it is high time that we also recognized that the 'tyranny' of Richard II and the victory of Henry V alike were in this connection mere incidental

[12] Ibid. 368(75).

[13] Ibid. iv.63–4(5).

[14] Ibid. v.228–30(8,9,10).

[15] Edward IV's grant for life was made late in his second parliament (in 1465). Richard III's was the first to be made to any king in his first parliament (1484), but this then became the invariable practice until, in his first parliament (1625), Charles I was granted tonnage and poundage for only one year. (Charles continued to levy it all the same.)

breezes playing on a stream of development which was flowing quite independently of them both. That stream of development was the growing realization in parliament—and I emphasize in parliament—that the King's revenue was no longer adequate to his permanent needs. Any amplification had to be achieved, in practice, by a parliamentary grant. But if a parliamentary grant were made permanent it would never need to be renewed, and would therefore cease being regarded as something—in parliament's own words—'proceeding from the free and spontaneous grant of Lords and Commons', which was the view of the matter that parliament was evidently anxious to enforce. Here, then, were two divergent needs: the needs of the King demanded that his standing revenue be permanently amplified; the needs of parliament demanded that the amplification should (as parliament put it) be 'interrupted' from time to time, in order that it might thereby become the subject of a fresh grant. The two divergent needs were reconciled by making grants for the King's life: this met the need for permanence by providing, not indeed *absolute* permanence, but permanence of a relative kind, permanence so far as the reigning King was concerned; at the same time, since a life-grant was automatically extinguished by the reigning King's death, parliament was still left with recurring opportunities of making fresh grants at each succession to the throne.

We may now turn away from indirect taxation and ask: How did the parliaments of our period handle direct taxation? The broad answer is that the two stories stand in contrast. As we have seen, parliament's grants of indirect taxation formed a sequence that was continuous, each successive grant being dovetailed into its predecessor. Parliament's grants of direct taxation, on the other hand, were as a whole discontinuous, in the sense that they left intervals of years during which no direct taxation fell due. The longest of those intervals were the ten years 1361–70, and the seven years 1423–9; the rest were mostly intervals of two years, though there were a few intervals of a single year. On the other hand, we must never forget that there were also stretches of time during which direct taxes of greater or lesser amount fell due *in a series of consecutive years*. The longest of these stretches were the fourteen years 1407–20, the eleven years 1344 to 1354, and the nine years 1430–8. The rest were mostly stretches of three or four years. During these stretches direct taxes fell due every year. But the broad contrast with indirect taxation is sufficiently obvious: indirect taxation continuous; direct taxation discontinuous.

Now the story of parliamentary grants of direct taxation during our period revolves around one tax. The overwhelming majority of the grants of direct taxation were grants of tax known as the Fifteenth and Tenth. The name 'Fifteenth and Tenth' commemorated the fact that the tax had originally been an impost assessed on every man's moveable property, but by our period it had ceased to be a tax assessed each time on every man's moveables; and had become a stereotyped charge apportioned in fixed quotas upon each township and borough of every shire, but based upon the amounts that each had paid when the tax had been assessed on moveables in 1334. Thus, Bedfordshire was always liable for a stereotyped sum of £674 and some odd shillings, towards which each township and borough in the county had to contribute a known and stereotyped quota. From the kingdom as a whole, 'one entire fifteenth and tenth' produced a fixed sum, which in round figures was £38,000. Places which suffered some temporary disaster or devastation could have their quota temporarily adjusted, but broadly speaking the Exchequer saw to it that such adjustments were kept temporary, and that the stereotyped quota was in due course restored. As might be expected, such a stereotyped assessment tended to get out of line with the actual distribution of wealth in the country: some places became wealthier and others less wealthy, but their quotas remained fixed. The only real remedy, of course, would have been a periodical reassessment of the whole country, but reassessment, then as now, was a laborious business from the government's point of view, and was evidently suspected by the taxpayers. 'Better to bear those ills we have, than fly to others we know not of.' So a system which had originally been intended as a temporary device became a fixture: but with all its anomalies it had, for government and taxpayers alike, one great merit—it avoided uncertainties. Nevertheless it bristled with anomalies.

The granting of fifteenths and tenths was not by any means a simple matter. Parliament had not only to decide how many fifteenths and tenths it would grant on each occasion—it sometimes granted as many as three, but more frequently it granted two or one or some fraction of a fifteenth and tenth: two fifteenths and tenths equal £76,000; half a fifteenth and tenth equals £19,000; 1⅓ fifteenths and tenths equal just over £50,000. Parliament also had to decide on each occasion another matter of considerable practical importance, both to the government and to the taxpayers—how the payment of the tax was to be spread, how many instalments, and of what amounts. For instance, quite a common form of grant was one entire fifteenth and tenth to be paid in two equal instalments at two due dates spaced equally over a year. But there were many variations of that pattern. Thus in 1392 we have a grant of 1½ fifteenths and tenths, the half due at Easter, and the one at Midsummer, only three months later.[16] In 1420, on the other hand, there is a grant of 1⅓ fifteenths and tenths, the one due on 2 February, and the third due on 11 November, nine months later.[17] As you see, the possible permutations were numerous, and there were in fact more of these permutations in the grants of direct taxation than there were even in the grants of indirect taxation. These variations involved precise matters like rates of tax, sums of money, due dates, and a variety of considerations like the needs of the government and the convenience of the taxpayers—none of which could be left to chance. I do not forget, of course, that the English are said to have acquired an empire in a fit of absent-mindedness—or so I used to be taught here in Oxford (though the epigram was imported from Cambridge)—but that was much later than our period! It was not in fits of absent-mindedness that English parliaments of the fourteenth and fifteenth centuries drew up their numerous, precise, and constantly varying grants of taxation to the King.

I have said that the story of parliamentary grants of direct taxation during our period revolves round the fifteenth and tenth. There were, however, two spells during which parliament had recourse to other and unusual forms of direct taxes. The first of

---

[16] *Rot. Parl.* iii.285–6(10).   [17] Ibid. iv.117(8).

these two spells was in the decade 1371–80.[18] The second was longer-drawn, being spread over the earlier half of the fifteenth century.

Between 1371 and 1380 the unusual direct taxes to which parliament had recourse were four in number: they consisted of what might be called a parish levy, granted in 1371, and three poll taxes, granted respectively in 1377, 1379, and 1380. On the whole, these four grants have had a bad press among historians—largely, I think, because the first of them, the parish levy of 1371, had a rather unfortunate beginning, while the last of them, the poll tax of 1380, had a tragic ending in the Peasants' Revolt of 1381. From our point of view, I think that the parish levy of 1371 is worth a little 'close-up'. The recent reopening of the Hundred Years War required that a large sum of money be raised quickly. Parliament decided that the sum should be £50,000, and that it should be raised by the unusual expedient of what I have called a parish levy.[19] The sum of money that had to be produced, £50,000, was divided by the total number of parishes in England. The quotient gave an *average* amount that would be contributed by all parishes, irrespective of their population or wealth. That average amount, however, was to be used only as a notional figure in making the actual assessment. When the commissioners came to make the actual assessment, they were instructed to vary the notional average 'so that', to quote the terms of the grant, 'each parish of greater value shall be proportionately aiding to another parish of lesser value'. In itself, this was a perfectly reasonable procedure, provided that the notional average was reasonably correct. Now the notional average specified in the grant made by parliament on 28 March 1371 was 22s. 3d. per parish. That figure had evidently been arrived at on the supposition that there were nearly 45,000 parishes in England. That supposition was of course quite absurd, and the whole episode has moved historians, some to astonishment,

---

[18] On the direct taxation of the decade, see also Charles Oman, *The Great Revolt of 1381*, ed. E. B. Fryde (Oxford, 1969), pp. xii–xix. On the subject of parliamentary taxation of the period in general, see G. L. Harriss, *King, Parliament and Public Finance in Medieval England to 1369* (Oxford, 1975).

[19] *Rot. Parl.* ii.303–4(6).

others to ridicule, others to contempt, and all alike to varying
attributions of blame. Within a month of the making of the grant
on 28 March the King's ministers had realized that the assumed
figure of 45,000 parishes was wildly wrong, so each sheriff was
commanded to send back one of the two knights of the shire and
one of the two burgesses who had served for each shire and
borough in the parliament which had made the grant to attend an
assembly at Winchester on 8 June to reconsider the grant: mean-
while each sheriff was also ordered to certify the King of the
number of parishes in his shire.[20] When the assembly met at
Winchester, the Chancellor explained that the certificate furnished
by the sheriffs and also by the bishops, showed that the number of
parishes in England was not so great as the last parliament had
supposed.[21] After the new information had been considered, the
assembly decided that the notional average per parish must be
raised from 22s. 3d. to 116s.,[22] which implies that the certified
number of parishes was just over 8,600. In making the revised
grant, it was once again emphatically prescribed that 'the parishioners of each parish of greater value shall be aiding and contributory to the parishioners of the parishes of lesser value'.

Now admittedly this was not a good beginning, but at any rate
the error was quite quickly corrected, and therefore we should not
allow the astonishment or ridicule or contempt of historians—
natural as they are—to distract us from asking one question. We
are watching a machine at work, and you can't watch attentively
if you are shaking with laughter or bursting with contempt. In
adopting this parish levy in 1371, what was our machine, what was
parliament trying to do? It had to find the considerable sum of
£50,000. Now as one fifteenth and tenth produced £38,000, a
grant of 1⅓ fifteenths and tenths, would have produced almost
exactly the right sum. Parliament sometimes granted precisely
1⅓ fifteenths and tenths—it did so in 1419, for instance.[23] If in
1419, why not also in 1371? Why in 1371 did parliament turn
away from the long-established fifteenth and tenth and adopt this

[20] *Report from the Lord's Committees . . . for all Matters Touching the Dignity of a
Peer* (London, 1820–9), iv.650–2.
[21] *Rot. Parl.* ii.304(10).   [22] Ibid. (11).   [23] Ibid. iv.117(8).

new-fangled parish levy? 'Turn away', did I say? In 1371, the fifteenth and tenth had not been levied in England for ten consecutive years. 'Keep away' is what I ought to have said: parliament evidently adopted the parish levy of 1371 because it wished to keep away from the fifteenth and tenth, if that was possible. Why? The reason is indicated quite clearly by the repeated emphasis upon the point that in assessing the parish levy 'the parishes of greater value should be aiding and contributory to the parishes of lesser value', in other words that the stronger should aid the weaker. For as we have seen, that was precisely what did *not* happen with the fifteenth and tenth: there, the strong did not aid the weak, the strong *could* not aid the weak, for weak and strong alike were held to their fixed quotas.

The parish levy of 1371 was followed by the three poll taxes of 1377, 1379, and 1380.[24] Specially interesting from our point of view is the last, the poll tax of 1380. The poll tax of 1380 was calculated on exactly the same principle as the parish levy of 1371, except, of course, that the taxable unit in 1380 was the individual person, whereas in 1371 it had been the individual parish. Just as in 1371 the assessment had been calculated from a notional average per parish, with the parishes of greater value proportionately aiding those of lesser value; so also in 1380, the assessment of the poll tax was calculated from a notional average of three groats per person, with 'the strong aiding the weak', ('le fort aidant al feable'), as they expressed it,[25] subject only to the limitations that the 'weak' should not pay less than one groat, nor the 'strong' more than sixty groats. As you see, the *principle* of 'the strong aiding the weak' is exactly the same in both taxes. In 1380 there can be no possible doubt that parliament deliberately chose the poll tax in preference to fifteenths and tenths, for the parliament roll of that year specifically records the fact that parliament did so, and explains that fifteenths and tenths were regarded as 'being very grievous to the Commons in many ways'. In other words, parliament regarded fifteenths and tenths as an unsatisfactory form of taxation, and in the 1370s was experimenting to try to find a

[24] Ibid. ii.364(19); iii.57–8(13–17), 90(15).
[25] Alternatively, 'les suffisantz . . . eidant les meindres'.

substitute for the fifteenth and tenth. Its experiments in that
decade happened to be brought to an end by the Peasants' Revolt
of 1381, but that consideration does not lessen the significance of
the fact that parliament made the experiments, and that its purpose
in making them was both conscious and reasonable. I'm not saying
that the principle of the strong helping the weak was satisfactorily
observed in practice. And we must remember that the position
was made much more difficult in 1380 because an unusually large
sum of money was required. The *diagnosis* was right even if the
remedy was not very satisfactory.

I have said that there was a second spell in our period during
which parliament had recourse to novel forms of direct taxation:
this was spread over the first half of the fifteenth century. Some of
these grants are so curiously complicated that they are difficult to
follow—in fact one of them, made in 1431,[26] was actually can-
celled in the next parliament[27] because of the ambiguities and
doubts which it raised! For our present purposes, however, I
think that two general points stand out.

(i) most of these fifteenth century experiments in parliamentary
taxation were taxes on *income*, and became progressively heavier
and more searching between 1404 and 1449; and

(ii) these new direct taxes seem to have been largely occasioned
by a significant development in connection with the fifteenth and
tenth. We have seen that parliament had failed to find an acceptable substitute for the fifteenth and tenth during the 1370s: if the
poll tax ever had any chance of taking the place of the fifteenth
and tenth, that chance was blasted for ever by the Peasants'
Revolt. So the fifteenth and tenth remained with all its inequities.
In the 1430s parliament tackled this problem in another way. The
parliament of 1433 began the practice of granting the fifteenth and
tenth subject to a stated deduction, which was to be applied proportionately to reduce the quotas due from places which had
decayed. The deduction stipulated in 1433 was £4,000 from every
entire fifteenth and tenth,[28] and this deduction was repeated in
subsequent grants of a fifteenth and tenth until 1445, when it was

[26] *Rot. Parl.* iv.369–70(15).   [27] Ibid. 409–10(50).   [28] Ibid. 425(20).

put up to £6,000 from every entire fifteenth and tenth.[29] In other words, from 1433 onwards the value of one entire fifteenth and tenth was dropped from £38,000 to £34,000, and from 1445 onwards to £32,000. So the taxes on income introduced by parliament during the earlier half of the fifteenth century were in effect *supplementary to* the fifteenth and tenth, which was then declining in productiveness owing to the deductions made by parliament from 1433 onwards: but those deductions were necessitated by the inequities of the fifteenth and tenth.

I am conscious, Ladies and Gentlemen, that in this lecture today I have punished you a great deal, not merely with detail, but with detail of a technical and perhaps rather repulsive kind. However, we here are supposed to be watching a machine at work, and we cannot watch a machine intelligently without attending to at least a few of the technical details. Next time, we might try to consider the bearing of some of these technical details upon some of the broader questions about parliament during our period.

[29] Ibid. v.69(15).

LECTURE 3

Taxation II

I BEGAN the last lecture with the point that the second century of
the English parliament coincided almost exactly with the period of
the Hundred Years War, with the consequence that urgent
financial business was constantly arising in parliament. We might
therefore begin the present lecture by asking: How did parliament
answer the financial challenges of the Hundred Years War? So far
as I can make out, the answer which traditionally passes current—
not expressly formulated, but apparently taken as being self-
evident—is that parliament's basic attitude to taxation during our
period was one of 'resistance'; that it made grants of taxation with
'reluctance'; and that when it did make grants, they were apt to be
'niggardly'. The words 'resistance', 'reluctance', 'niggardly' are
not mine: I am quoting all three.[1] Are they a sound description of
parliament's attitude to taxation? My answer would be that they
are highly misleading, if the facts are considered as a whole.

They are especially misleading in connection with indirect
taxation, which in our period, we must remember, formed a very
valuable and important slice of the King's revenue. Now parliament certainly objected to the subsidy on wool, as also to tonnage
and poundage, and resisted all three—*but only when they were
granted by the merchants*. As we saw last time, when the granting of
the subsidy on wool, for instance, was in parliament's own hands,

---

[1] 'Resistance' is the word used by Eileen Power in *The Wool Trade in English
Medieval History* (Oxford, 1941), p. 82; 'reluctance' by H. G. Richardson and
George Sayles, in 'The Parliaments of Edward III', *Bulletin of the Institute of
Historical Research* (*B.I.H.R.*), vol. ix (1931–2), p. 15; and 'niggardly' by T. F.
Tout, in *Chapters in the Administrative History of Medieval England* (Manchester,
1920–33). Although Sir Goronwy made this last attribution in a marginal note,
he gave no volume or page reference, and a search for the word in the *Chapters*
has not availed.

as it was from 1351 onwards, it was granted in a continuous sequence, each grant—for the most part—being made before the expiry of the previous grant. On no occasion did parliament after 1351 *refuse* to grant the wool subsidy. Only on a few occasions, and then only for brief spells—at any rate down to the end of Henry V's reign—did parliament grant the wool subsidy at low rates: mostly it was at the highest rate. This does not in the least mean that parliament granted it as a matter of course. In 1351, for instance, when protesting against the subsidy's being granted by the merchants, parliament indicated that it would be prepared to consider granting it for half a year or a whole year if the King could show cause: the King showed cause, and evidently made a good case, for parliament granted the subsidy—not for half a year or one year as it had said, but for two whole years. Again in 1378, parliament began by asking to be excused from making any grant at all, because of the heavy taxes that had recently been paid and because of the losses caused by cattle plague and the French raids on the south coast;[2] but after one of the King's ministers had explained the situation, and had shown what had happened to the money previously granted,[3] parliament granted that the current subsidy on wool, which was not due to expire till September 1379, should be continued for another six months from that date (i.e. to Easter 1380), *plus* an additional *13s. 4d.* per sack of wool from Easter 1379 to Easter 1380.[4] On both occasions, as you see, parliament showed itself prepared to listen to argument. So far therefore as indirect taxation is concerned, the evidence seems to me to be quite clearly contrary to the supposition that parliament showed 'resistance' or 'reluctance' or 'niggardliness' in making its grants: parliaments did insist that cause be shown, which was neither 'resistance' nor 'reluctance' but plain common sense; and it did listen to the argument when cause was shown.

Direct taxation might at first sight seem to be in a different case. Direct taxation certainly was not granted in continuous sequence, like indirect taxation, and there were occasions when parliament declined to grant direct taxation, though by no means all of these

[2] *Rot. Parl.* iii.35(18).   [3] Ibid. 35-6(19-21).   [4] Ibid. 37-8(29).

were flat refusals; thus the parliament of November 1381 declined to grant any direct taxation, but on the reasonable ground that it would be politically inexpedient to do so while the country was still unsettled after the Peasants' Revolt;[5] a year later, however, when the crisis was past, parliament reverted again to direct taxation in the form of a fifteenth and tenth. The statement—or insinuation—that the parliamentary grants of direct taxation to meet the expenses of the Hundred Years War were 'niggardly' seems to me to have little value as an objective judgment, because it ignores at least two considerations of practical and capital importance. On the one hand, there are a good many signs that the government was often unable to give parliament any serviceable estimates of the amounts that were required. And on the other hand, there seems to be little doubt that when once the war became prolonged, England's resources were not sufficient to carry on the struggle and that the burden of taxation became extremely heavy for the taxpayer. All these points are well illustrated by what happened in the parliament of November 1380.

In his opening speech, the Chancellor declared that 'a very large sum' was needed, and must be raised quickly, to provide for the immediate needs of defence and of the war which were specified.[6] He was pressed to state 'clearly' what was the total sum required. In response to that pressure the government estimated that a grant of £160,000 was needed.[7] (We must jog our modern minds to remember that £160,000, especially if it was raised quickly, as it had to be on that occasion, was a very large sum in the circumstances of those days—a very large sum indeed.) After much negotiation and discussion, parliament agreed to a grant of £100,000, of which two-thirds (£66,000) would be found by the laity, and one-third by the clergy.[8] Now if £160,000 was a sound estimate of what was really required—and nobody seems to have suggested that it was not sound—then without doubt a grant of as much as a third less was inadequate. But whether it was also 'niggardly' seems to me to depend upon parliament's reason for refusing the full amount. What was the reason?

[5] Ibid. 104(36).   [6] Ibid. 88(4).   [7] Ibid. 89(10–11).   [8] Ibid. 90(13–15).

According to the parliament roll,[9] the reason for not agreeing
to the full £160,000 was that such a sum was 'moelt outrageouse
et oultrement importable . . . a la Commune'—very enormous
and utterly unbearable to the Commons. 'But', you say, 'that is not
a reason: it is just a flat refusal, with no reason given.' Not quite,
I think. 'Importable'—unbearable—is in this context quite a precise word. If a tax is truly 'importable', the taxpayers will refuse to
pay, or will somehow evade payment. Suppose that in 1380 the
full amount of £160,000 had been agreed to by parliament. In that
case, we may very probably assume that the clergy would have
had to find a third of it, and that the laity would have had to find
two-thirds, i.e. £106,000. Would a sum of £106,000, levied
quickly, have been 'utterly unbearable to the Commons' in 1380?
We can test it by what actually happened. The grant to which
parliament actually agreed was £100,000, of which the laity had
to find £66,000.[10] To produce that sum, parliament imposed a
poll tax, calculated on a notional average of three groats per person,
'the strong aiding the weak', payment to be in two instalments
within the short period of five months. The result is well known:
large-scale evasions, culminating in the Peasants' Revolt of 1381.
If the laity had had to produce, not two-thirds of £100,000, but
two-thirds of £160,000, the rate of tax would have had to be, not
three groats, but nearly five groats per person. And that presumably would have led to evasions on a larger scale still. We must
remember that the ten previous years had been a decade of heavy
taxation and unrelieved disaster. So parliament was clearly
justified in 1380 in asserting that £160,000 would be 'utterly
unbearable to the Commons'. That being so, its refusal to agree to
the full £160,000 cannot reasonably be regarded as 'niggardly':
besides, the niggard's way is to give as little as he can; but in
agreeing to the £100,000 parliament in 1380 was granting, not as
little as it could, but as much as it dared. And the event showed
that it had dared to grant more than a great many of the taxpayers
in 1380 were prepared to bear.

I have dwelt on this point, and taken it with particular reference
to the difficult year 1380, not from any concern about the appro-

[9] Ibid. 89(12).   [10] Ibid. 90(13).

priateness of the word 'niggardly', but because a question of much
greater substance is involved. It is the question which I asked a
moment ago: How did parliament answer the financial challenge
of the Hundred Years War? The evidence taken together and
viewed as a whole seems to me to indicate that parliament's *basic*
attitude towards taxation was not one of 'resistance' but of
reasonable co-operation. *Reasonable* co-operation: the government
had to show cause, and not infrequently found itself straitly
questioned in course of doing so. But if cause was shown, parliament's *basic* tendency in taxation was to co-operate, to co-operate
reasonably. And we must remember, after all, that its right of
consenting to taxation was gained by *giving* consent, not by withholding it, and by giving it repeatedly, by withholding it but
rarely.

We may now turn to a different question. What demands did
this granting of taxation make upon the activity and initiative of
parliament? This is a question much easier to ask than to answer,
but we must ask it, because we are trying to watch the machine at
work. We saw last time that grants of taxation, whether of direct
or of indirect taxation, could not be made in fits of absent-
mindedness: the grants involved too many precise details which
had to be consciously thought out and fitted together. Who did
the thinking out and the fitting together?

As Stubbs pointed out long ago, parliamentary grants of
taxation—I mean the documentary instruments by which the
grants were made—purported to be joint acts of Lords and
Commons: down to the 1390s, grants of money were described
simply as being made 'by the Lords and Commons'; from the
1390s onwards, they were described more specifically as being
made 'by the Commons with the assent of the Lords'.[11] Stubbs
duly pointed out also that the method by which these joint grants
of taxation were arrived at was through the conferences of Lords
and Commons[12] which—as we have already seen—were an

[11] The transition to the later formula occurred during the period 1383–95.
Cf. *Rot. Parl.* iii.151(13), 285(10), 301(11), 330(6).

[12] William Stubbs, *The Constitutional History of England* (4th edn., Oxford,
1906), ii.623.

important feature of medieval parliamentary procedure in England. Clearly, then, the process of thinking out and fitting together involved at least two participants—the Lords and the Commons. Ordinary experience, and the very nature of the practical problems of taxation, further suggest that we should at least inquire about a possible third participating party—the King's ministers and officers.

Now the legal position of the *Commons* in parliament was that they were the accredited attorneys of the shires and boroughs which they represented, endowed with full legal powers to bind their respective constituencies to do whatever should be ordained by common counsel in parliament.[13] The legal position of the *Lords* in parliament was that they were all summoned as individuals, and represented nobody but themselves and their own villeins. The King's government, from Edward I's time onwards, had attached great practical importance to the representatives' legal power of making grants of taxation which were legally binding upon the taxpayers. In the sphere of taxation, therefore, there was a very real sense in which the Commons could be regarded as of greater power, and of greater importance to the government, than the Lords: for if the government attached any importance to obtaining a legally binding consent to taxation, they could not get it from the Lords; only the Commons had the legal power to give it to them. The relative importance in the eyes of the government of Lords and Commons so far as the granting of taxation was concerned is well illustrated by what happened in 1371. In that year, as we saw last time,[14] parliament made the experiment of granting a new form of direct taxation which I described as a parish levy. They had to raise £50,000, and acting on the mistaken idea that England contained nearly 45,000 parishes, they fixed the notional average contribution per parish at 22s. 3d. When the mistake was realized, a number of those who had attended the parliament which had made the mistaken grant were summoned to come

[13] J. G. Edwards, 'The *Plena Potestas* of English Parliamentary Representatives', *Oxford Essays in Medieval History presented to Herbert Edward Salter* (Oxford, 1934), and also *Historical Studies of the English Parliament*, ed. E. B. Fryde and E. Miller (Cambridge, 1970), vol. 1.

[14] See above, pp. 27-9

back to another assembly at Winchester to reconsider and revise
the grant of taxation that parliament had made: this they did, and
in the light of the more accurate information about the number of
parishes supplied in the meantime by the sheriffs and the bishops,
they raised the average contribution per parish from the original
figure of 22s. 3d. to the figure of 116s. per parish.[15]

Now to the parliament which had made the original and
erroneous grant the King had summoned twenty bishops, twenty-
six abbots, eleven earls, fifty-one barons, and two representatives
from each county and parliamentary borough.[16] To the revising
assembly at Winchester he summoned four bishops (instead of
twenty), four abbots (instead of twenty-six), seven earls (instead of
eleven), six barons (instead of fifty-one), but from *every* shire one
of the two representatives which each shire had elected for the
original parliament, and from *every* parliamentary borough one
of the two representatives whom each borough had likewise
elected for the original parliament.[17] In short, one-in-five of the
Lords, but one-in-two of the Commons, and that one-in-two
drawn from every constituency. In other words, a one-in-two
selection of those who mattered most, and only a one-in-five
selection of those who mattered less, i.e. for the business in hand,
which on that occasion was pre-eminently taxation. The incident
illustrates very clearly *where* the government thought that the
power of granting taxation resided, and *how* they thought it was
distributed, as between Lords and Commons.

The relation between Lords and Commons in taxation is more
specifically illustrated by the granting of the poll tax of 1380, to
which I already referred in another connection earlier in this
lecture:[18] I refer to it again because it happens to be the only
reasonably full account in the parliament rolls of the procedure
that was followed in making such grants. The government, as we
have seen, told parliament that the urgent needs of defence and
of the war required the speedy raising of the very large sum of

---

[15] *Rot. Parl.* ii.303–4(6,10,11).
[16] *Report . . . touching the Dignity of a Peer*, iv. 646–9.
[17] Ibid. 650–3.
[18] See above, pp. 34–5

£160,000. The Commons, after discussion among themselves, answered that such a sum was 'importable', and asked that it be reduced to some figure that would be 'portable'. They also asked the Lords to consider the ways by which they thought that such a 'portable' sum could be raised. The Lords were evidently not ready for this, for they did not answer until after they had had what the parliament roll calls 'a long discussion'. But after having this long discussion among themselves, the Lords told the Commons that they thought that there were three possible ways of raising the money. One was by means of a poll tax, calculated on a notional average of so many groats per person, 'the strong aiding the weak'. If, however, that way was not acceptable to the Commons, another way would be by means of a tax of so much in the pound on the value of all merchandise sold within the kingdom, and the third way would be to grant as many fifteenths and tenths as were necessary to produce the required sum. The Lords then added some comments. The fifteenths and tenths, they said, were for several reasons 'very grievous to the poor' taxpayers —(reasons which we saw last time). The sales tax on merchandise, they remarked, would be slow in coming in, and nobody could be sure how much it would produce. So their view was that the poll tax would be the best way, as it would fall on everybody, and could be paid by everybody 'provided that the strong are compelled to help the weak': they added that a notional average of four or five groats per person, the strong helping the weak, would produce the required sum.[19]

Well eventually, as we have seen, the Commons after much discussion accepted the suggestion of a poll tax, but insisted that £160,000 would be 'importable', and must be cut to £100,000, of which the clergy must find a third. The Commons then fixed the rate for the laity at three groats per person, the strong helping the weak, and no one paying more than sixty groats or less than one groat (4d.). The point that comes out clearly in all this is that in taxation the role of the Lords was one of advice, and they did not offer even advice until the Commons had asked for it. The choice, the decision, which method of taxation should be adopted

[19] *Rot. Parl.* iii.89–90(11–14).

and at what rate, was left to the Commons; it was the Commons
who insisted on the cut from the 'unbearable' total sum of
£160,000 to £100,000; it was the Commons who finally decided
that the notional average rate per person should be three groats,
the strong helping the weak, not the four or five groats indicated
by the Lords; and it was the Commons who prescribed a maxi-
mum contribution of sixty groats and a minimum contribution of
one groat.

And now how about the King's ministers and officers: what
part are we to suppose that they took in parliament's granting of
taxation? Well, it is of course clear that the Chancellor, or whoever delivered the 'charge', often devoted a part of his speech to
explaining the King's financial necessities. It is also clear that royal
ministers or officers supplied financial information in parliament,
sometimes to the Lords and the Commons' delegates in the White
Chamber, sometimes to the general body of the Commons in
their own separate meeting place: such occasions are mentioned in
the parliament rolls from time to time,[20] and we may reasonably
presume that they quite probably occurred more frequently than
they are actually recorded in the parliament rolls. What is not
clear, however, is the extent to which royal ministers and officers
—particularly those who were officially concerned with finance—
supplied guidance, criticisms or suggestions while grants of taxation were being discussed and worked out. It is reasonable to
suppose, for instance, that the many variations in the instalments
and due dates of direct taxes may well have been arranged after
consultations with the Exchequer. On the other hand, what are we
to make of the King's ministers and officers in relation to the
parish levy of 1371, when parliament fell into the error of sup-
posing that there were nearly 45,000 parishes in England, the real
number being between eight and nine thousand?

The last point that I want to touch upon before leaving the
subject of taxation is this: What was the legal importance of

[20] e.g. Richard, lord Scrope, the steward of the King's Household, in 1378
undertook to give the Commons such information, only grudgingly however
(ibid. 36(21)). In January 1380, when he was chancellor, it was done voluntarily
(ibid. 71(5)).

parliament's granting of taxation? I say 'legal' importance, and not 'constitutional' importance, because the 'constitutional' importance of parliamentary taxation has often been discussed, whereas its *legal* importance is a much less familiar topic, and seems to me to be a topic that deserves more attention than it usually receives.

For our purposes, I think that it is necessary to be much more specific than Stubbs, for instance, needed to be about the documentary instrument by which the parliamentary grants of taxation were made. What form did that instrument take? It would be natural, I suppose, to expect that these grants would take the form of a statute, and the fact that some of them are sometimes recited incidentally in the Statute Rolls, and consequently appear in the printed edition of the *Statutes of the Realm*, might seem to bear out that expectation. In fact, however, parliamentary grants of taxation during our period did not take the form of a statute: the form that they took was that of an indenture. The indenture was a very common and very ancient form of document which was used when circumstances required that a legal instrument should exist in two or more identical exemplars: in a contract, for instance, each of the parties to the contract needs an exemplar for himself. In order to provide a simple test of the identity of the exemplars, they wrote the two or more copies that were required on a single piece of parchment, and then cut them apart by a zig-zag cut. This left a zig-zag edge to each of the exemplars, and if their identity and genuineness were disputed, they could easily be tested by seeing whether the zig-zag edges fitted into one another. As these edges looked like teeth, the documents so cut were said to be 'indented'. Hence the name 'indenture'. A grant of taxation by parliament was drawn up in that 'indented' form. We must presume that—originally at any rate—two exemplars of each grant were made, one being handed to the King, and the other presumably being retained by parliament. By our period, a summary or a full transcript of these indentures was enrolled in the parliament roll. The actual indentures that were handed to the King have mostly disappeared, though a few of them have managed to survive.

Now there are two important legal points for us to notice about the subsidy-indenture.

(i) The subsidy-indenture was in itself and by itself an absolutely authoritative legal document, on the strength of which, without more ado, the King proceeded to take the administrative action necessary to collect the tax granted by the indenture. 'The tax granted by the indenture.' The indenture did not *offer* the tax to the King, it *granted* the tax to him. And the grant was binding on the King's subjects: if any subject refused or neglected to pay his due share of the tax that was granted, the courts would compel him to pay, just as they would if necessary compel him to observe a statute, or any other part of the law of England. In other words, although the subsidy-indenture was not a statute, it was within its ambit binding law, as authoritative and binding as a statute.

(ii) Whereas a statute was made by the King in response (broadly speaking) to a petition from Lords or Commons, the subsidy-indenture was made 'by Lords and Commons' ('by the Commons with the assent of the Lords' from the 1390s onwards) *in response to a request from the King*: it was their 'answer' to the request for an aid made on the King's behalf in the 'charge' delivered at the initial assembling of the parliament. When I was dealing with that initial assembly in the first lecture, you may remember that I remarked then that the Commons attended parliament not only as petitioners but also as 'answerers'.[21] We can now amplify that point by adding two particulars. Firstly, that in the sphere of taxation, the 'answers' which the Commons shared in framing were not mere expressions of opinion about this or that: some of the 'answers' were expressions of opinion in the sphere of taxation, and the answers in which the Commons participated were authoritative and binding decisions, by which all the King's subjects were legally bound. Secondly, that in the sphere of taxation, the Commons not merely 'shared' in making the grants—they might have 'shared' in no more than an inferior sort of way—but actually they 'shared' this function with the Lords *not* as 'inferiors', but as having equal authority, and in practice often more than equal authority, alongside the Lords. This is a point that needs to

[21] See above, pp. 3-4

be emphasized, because it has often been overlooked by those who regard the role of the Commons in medieval parliaments as having been predominantly that of 'petitioners'. That view expresses only a part of the truth. The *whole* truth is that the Commons were not only petitioners, but just as much, especially from the King's point of view, 'answerers' as well: as 'petitioners' they were, in one sense, 'inferior' to the Lords; but as 'answerers', particularly in the very important sphere of taxation, their authority was in every sense equal to that of the Lords. We shall be coming back to that point at a later stage. In the meantime we shall be considering Petitions and Bills.

Petitions and Bills I

WE must now turn to the subject of Petitions and Bills in parliament during our period. That petitions and bills were a standing and important item in the business of parliament is clear from two facts that I have already mentioned in passing.

(i) We have seen that in the initial assembling of parliament, the 'charge' not only stated the 'points' about which the King wanted 'answers', but also announced the King's willingness to receive and answer petitions;[1]

(ii) That in almost every parliament roll of our period, there is a section devoted to what are called 'Petitions des Communes' or 'Communes petitions', the section which (as I explained before[2]) comes last in each parliament roll; and in quite a number of parliament rolls, that section devoted to Common Petitions occupies greater space than any other section, and not infrequently occupies even greater space than the other sections put together. So, of the various products of the parliamentary machine, petitions and bills were at any rate the most numerous, and for that reason alone would demand our attention, since we are watching the machine at work. But they demand our attention also as historians, because they have significant light to throw on the development of parliament, as well as on its working.

Perhaps I may explain just in passing why I say 'petitions and bills', not just 'petitions' by itself or 'bills' by itself. I do so because it is important to realize quite clearly that the terms 'petition' and 'bill', though not synonymous, are, for our purposes, *equivalent*

---

[1] See above, pp. 3-4
[2] See above, p. 17

terms. Until some twenty or thirty years ago[3] it was believed that
'petition' and 'bill' were quite different things, and that view therefore still appears in many books—some of them good books—
that are still in current use. The difference between 'petition' and
'bill' was supposed to be this. A 'petition' was supposed to be a
request pure and simple. A 'bill' was supposed to be a petition
drawn up in such a way that it not only stated a request, but also
supplied a draft of the actual remedy that was desired by the
petitioner. That petitions could be drawn up, and sometimes were
drawn up, in that way is certainly true. It is not true, however, that
petitions in that form were necessarily called 'bills' or that
petitions which were requests pure and simple were necessarily
called 'petitions'. Either form might be referred to as a 'petition'
or as a 'bill'. For our present purpose, therefore, the words
'petition' and 'bill' were equivalent terms. But they were not
strictly speaking synonymous terms. A 'bill' was always a *written*
thing, and the writing contained in it often made a request, and
was therefore in substance a petition, but a 'bill' was not necessarily a writing that made a request; it could be a writing that
made statements of various kinds, e.g. a statement of costs. On the
other hand, a petition was not always or necessarily a written

[3] That is, 'twenty or thirty years' prior to 1961 (the date of these Lectures).
A. F. Pollard was, and remained (*Evolution of Parliament*, 2nd edn. [London, 1926],
pp. 118–20, 127–9, 308), of the firm opinion that *communes petitions* were the work
of the House of Commons; and H. L. Gray in *The Influence of the Commons on
Early Legislation* (Harvard, 1932), while usefully disproving the idea that 'petition'
and 'bill' were different things, laid so much emphasis on Pollard's doctrine as to
translate *communes petitions* as 'commons' bills'. For this, as well as for his idea that
initiation of statutes by common petitions represented popular control of legislation, Gray was severely taken to task by S. B. Chrimes (*Constitutional Ideas in the
Fifteenth Century* [Cambridge, 1936], pp. 236–49, especially pp. 243–5.) Subsequently, Gray's interpretations and theory were also weighed and found sometimes wanting by A. R. Myers in 'Parliamentary Petitions in the Fifteenth
Century', *E.H.R.*, vol. LII (1937), pp. 385–404, 590–613, and especially by Doris
Rayner in 'The Forms and Machinery of the "Commune Petition" in the Fourteenth Century', *ibid.* LVI (1941), pp. 198–233, 549–70. It is interesting to note that
in a letter to James Tait of 1936 J. G. Edwards wrote of Miss Rayner's Manchester
Ph.D. thesis of 1934: 'After reading this thesis I felt, for my own part, that I
should not for the future assume that a *commune petition* was of necessity an
expression, in any effective sense, of any sort of collective opinion or desire of a
'house of commons'.'

thing—a petition in parliament could be made orally, but whether written or oral, a petition always made a request. So the words 'petition' and 'bill' were not in the strict sense synonymous. But for our present purpose they *were* equivalent terms. It is to emphasize their equivalence for our purpose that I have so far spoken of 'petitions and bills'. Having made that point clear, I shall now for convenience use the word 'petitions' by itself.

In the 'charge' delivered at the initial assembling of parliament, the announcement that the King was willing to receive and answer petitions was *general*, not particular. That is to say, it extended to all the King's subjects, not merely to the Lords and Commons who were present in parliament, and it applied both to grievances suffered by an individual person as well as to grievances suffered by a number of people or by people in general. Petitions about the grievances of an individual person were known by such descriptions as 'petitions of singular persons' (1352).[4] or 'especial bills of singular persons' (1350),[5] or 'petitions partielles', 'partial petitions' in the sense of 'petitions of a party', in the legal meaning of the word 'party'. The other kind of petition was known by such descriptions as 'petitions touching the Commons' (1348),[6] or 'petitions concerning grievances done to common people' (1352),[7] meaning by 'common people' not 'common' in the derogatory sense of 'the common herd', but 'common' in the sense opposite to 'singular persons'. That then was the basic classification of petitions presented in parliament: (1) 'petitions of singular persons', or 'singular petitions'; (2) 'petitions concerning grievances done to common people', or 'petitions touching the Commons' or 'common petitions'. For short: (1) singular petitions; (2) common petitions.

Now the singular petition was naturally put forward in the name of the singular person who wished to make the request, and as I have said, he could be any subject of the King, and need not be one of the Lords or Commons who was attending the parliament.

---

[4] *Rot. Parl.* ii.237(8).
[5] Ibid. 230(39).
[6] Ibid. 201(4). See Appendix, A, p. 80.
[7] Ibid. 237(8). See Appendix, B(i), p. 81.

The common petitions, on the other hand, because they were concerned with 'the grievances done to common people', i.e. people who were 'common' as distinct from people who were 'singular', were put forward by or in the name of the Commons who were attending the parliament: this was natural and logical, because the Commons were present in parliament as representatives of all the local communities of shire and borough, and they were therefore the obvious and most suitable mouthpieces for making known the 'grievances done to common people', the grievances done to people who were 'common' as distinct from people who were 'singular': the people who were 'singular' could—and did—speak each for himself in a singular petition.

The difference between singular and common petitions was reflected not only by the two different ways in which they were presented, but also by the two different ways in which they were disposed of. The singular petitions were handed in to the chancery clerks appointed to act as Receivers of petitions in the particular parliament.[8] These Receivers sorted them out, and passed them to the persons who had been named to act as Triers of petitions (or Auditors of petitions, as they were sometimes called) in the particular parliament. These Triers were named from among the Lords of parliament and the judges and other law officers of the King who were attending the parliament. The Triers disposed of the singular petitions in whatever way seemed appropriate, but any petitions that for some reason could not be settled without consulting the King were passed on by the Triers to the King and his council. The common petitions were handed to the Clerk of the Parliament,[9] who passed them on to the King and his council for decision. So the common petitions went as a matter of course to the King and his council, and were answered by the King and his council. The singular petitions did not go as a matter of course to the King and his council: they were answered by the Triers of petitions, unless the Triers decided that for some reason the petition in question could not be settled without consulting the

---

[8] e.g. ibid. 236(2) (1352). Cf. H. G. Richardson and George Sayles, art. cit., B.I.H.R. vol. ix (1931–2), p. 11. See Appendix, A, p. 81.

[9] *Rot. Parl.* ii.201(4). See Appendix, A, p. 80.

King—only in such cases were singular petitions sent on to be answered by the King and his council.

Now during the time of a parliament, 'the King and his council' meant 'the King and his council in parliament' i.e. the King and his council meeting in the White Chamber in company with the prelates and barons who had been individually summoned to attend the parliament. The common petitions, and those singular petitions that were sent on to the King by the Triers, were therefore considered by 'the council in parliament', i.e. by the King's continual counsellors together with the lords of parliament, and their advice on each petition was signified to the King, who had to make the final decision. There are indications that if the council and lords were of the opinion that the petition should be granted, they endorsed the petition with some such formula as 'This petition seems reasonable'; but if they thought that it should not be granted, they endorsed the petition to that effect, often with some indication of their reason. But in either case, whether the council and the lords approved or disapproved it, the common petition went to the King for final decision. So far as one can judge from rather scattered evidence, if the council and the lords disapproved of a petition, the King seems in practice to have refused it, but the decision lay with him, and the common petition was evidently submitted for his consideration even though the lords had disapproved it. In later times, of course, a bill sent up by the Commons and disapproved by the Lords was not submitted to the King for his consideration. 'A mere technicality', you say. A technicality—yes. A *mere* technicality—no. It is a technicality which is also a warning, a warning that the historical relation between the common petition of our period and the parliamentary bill of later times may not be so direct or so simple as is sometimes supposed. That point, however, is one to which we must return later.

Before we leave the various contrasts that existed between singular petitions and common petitions, there is one more that we must notice, because it is rather relevant to our purpose. If we compare the parliament rolls of our period with those that survive from the *first* century of the English parliament—and the best surviving specimen from that period is the parliament roll of 1305 that was so memorably edited by Maitland[10]—we shall be struck at once by a double-sided contrast. In the parliament rolls of our period, the common petitions are very numerous, and as I have already indicated, they are entered all together in one section of the parliament roll: their numbers varied quite widely from parliament to parliament, so an average would be misleading, but the total number of them enrolled in the parliament rolls for the hundred years or so, and the ninety parliaments or so, with which we are concerned, amounts to some 2,000; perhaps I might just add in passing that of this 2,000, some 400 belong to the parliaments which met during the decade of the 1370s, and another 250 or so come from the parliaments of the first decade of the fifteenth century. In the parliament roll of 1305, on the contrary, there was no section of common petitions classified as such, and the petitions which had a certain touch of 'common-ness', those from local communities of shire or borough, accounted for only about one in seven of the total number of petitions enrolled. That is one side of the double-sided contrast. The other side of the contrast is this. In the parliament rolls of our period, the number of singular petitions is small: during the earlier half of our period it is very small, but during the latter half it is somewhat greater; nevertheless, over our period as a whole, the small number of singular petitions enrolled in the parliament rolls is completely overshadowed by the great number of common petitions. In short: the petitions that bulk largest—by far the largest—in the parliament rolls of our period are the common petitions; in the parliament roll of 1305, on the other hand, the petitions that bulked largest—by far the largest—were the singular petitions. That is the broad contrast that we have to get quite clear in our minds. But having got the contrast clear, we must immediately add a rider. And the rider is this. When the numbers of singular petitions enrolled in the parliament rolls reach their lowest ebb, which is in the rolls of the *earlier* half of our period, it is precisely at that point that they take on a new significance in parliamentary history. And the first sign

[10] *Records of the Parliament at Westminster in 1305*, ed. F. W. Maitland (Rolls Series, 1893).

of their new significance is this: that in the *latter* half of our period, we find their number in the parliament rolls is, almost imperceptibly, but quite steadily, increasing. What does this mean? That question can be better answered, I think, if we first take another look at the common petitions.

We have already seen[11] that common petitions were 'petitions concerning grievances done to *common* people' as distinct from 'petitions of *singular* persons'. But we also saw[12] that whereas singular petitions were put forward in the name of the singular persons who were concerned in promoting them, the common petitions were put forward in the name of the Commons who were attending parliament as representatives of shires and boroughs. That is what the parliament rolls tell us. But when they say that common petitions were 'put forward by the Commons', what do the parliament rolls mean? Do they mean that the common petitions enrolled in the parliament rolls were put forward and vouched for by the Commons in some sort of corporate capacity, as in later times bills were put forward and vouched for by the Commons *as a body*? Or do the parliament rolls mean that common petitions were put forward by representatives, sometimes perhaps by a large group or even the general body of them, but sometimes also by only a small group of them, or even an individual representative among them? Clearly there is a big ambiguity here—an ambiguity which is of great practical importance to the historian.

Naturally, and perhaps almost inevitably, historians who are necessarily familiar with the later procedure, whereby bills put forward by the Commons are put forward by them in a corporate capacity, have been rather prone to conclude that in the fourteenth century, too, the common petitions were put forward by the Commons of those days in some sort of corporate capacity: even if in practice common petitions *originated* with groups, or even with some individual, among the representatives, the common petitions—it has often been supposed—would at any rate be 'avowed' by the general body of the Commons,[13] although

---

[11] See above, p. 46. [12] Ibid.

[13] Cf. Richardson and Sayles, art. cit., pp. 11–12. See Appendix, C, p. 83.

admittedly there is no record of the procedure by which this supposed 'avowal' was carried out. [14] Let us test this supposition by a document which happens to be very familiar in another connection.

In the parliament of 1372 there was promulgated the well known statute or ordinance (it is called by both names) which forbade the election as knights of the shire for parliament of sheriffs and of lawyers practising in the King's courts.[15] It is not clear why the statute was made just then, and anyway it seems—in regard to the lawyers—to have been more or less a dead letter, but the reason it gives for keeping the practising lawyers out of parliament is very interesting. The statute alleges that practising lawyers, when they are knights of the shire in parliament, 'cause to be put forward in parliament *in the name of the Commons* a number of petitions ('plusieurs petitions') which do not touch the Commons, but [touch] only the singular persons for whom the lawyers are acting'. A petition 'in the name of the Commons' obviously means a common petition, and the point of the complaint is that a *common* petition should not be used to forward the business of a *singular* person. Now unfortunately—though inevitably—it is not possible to identify any of these common petitions which these lawyers are alleged to have put forward in the interest of singular persons who were their clients: if the lawyers did what is alleged, any common petitions of that sort which they put forward would naturally not mention the singular persons whom they were intended to benefit. One may reasonably surmise, I think, that what the lawyers would probably do in these petitions would be either to ask in general terms for some change in the law or for some modification of legal procedure which would benefit or might be expected to benefit their client. And I would be inclined to guess further that some of the common petitions in which they unsuccessfully tried this on are probably among those that received the answers 'Let the common law take

---

[14] It is perhaps to be implied from the passage in Appendix C, under the date 1327, that 'avowal' on that occasion took the form of an indenture.

[15] *Rot. Parl.* ii.310(13). Cf. Richardson and Sayles, art. cit., p. 12. See Appendix C, pp. 83-4.

its course' or 'There is a statute: let it stand'. That, however, is only speculation: what matters is that we cannot now identify precisely any of the common petitions in which the lawyers played this game, so we don't know whether such petitions were many or few, and what is even more important, we don't know what sort of things they asked for. These various uncertainties, however, do not affect one point which specially concerns us here. It is this. Those who made that statute in 1372 evidently believed not merely that a lawyer who was one of the knights of the shire in parliament could put forward petitions 'in the name of the Commons' which 'did not touch the Commons at all': but also that there was no effective way of stopping this game except by prohibiting the election of practising lawyers as knights of the shire, and thus keeping them out of parliament altogether. But obviously the game could also have been stopped—or rather it would not have been played in the first instance—if the Commons, in any sort—in even the vaguest sort—of corporate capacity, had exercised any sort of effective scrutiny of the petitions that were put forward 'in the name of the Commons'.[16] It is therefore evident from the statute of 1372 that 'common petitions', petitions 'in the name of the Commons', could be put forward even by individual representatives among the Commons. This suggests that a common petition was not re- garded as something that was necessarily put forward by the Commons in a corporate capacity—though it sometimes might be.

The same point can be illustrated by an incidental sentence— which is significant precisely because it is incidental—in one of the common petitions presented in the parliament of 1379.[17] It deals with a subject which crops up from time to time in the common petitions of the fourteenth and fifteenth centuries. Occasionally it happened that the King and his council were not able to find time before the end of a parliament to answer all the common petitions

[16] It is interesting to note, in support of this statement, that in 1371 a common petition beginning 'Priount les . . . Communes qe . . .' was answered with 'Attende la venue des Communes' (*Rot. Parl.* ii.305(24)), and that when in 1394 two London chantry chaplains sued a bill before the King and Lords 'en les nouns des Com- munes', asking for a statute making bequests of tenements in the city effectual, the Commons objected to any such statute being passed (ibid. iii.321(44)).

[17] *Rot. Parl.* iii.61(28).

that had been presented. There was evidently some fear that this might happen in the 1379 parliament, for one of the Commons' petitions asked that 'petitions and bills put forward now in this present parliament, and all others which shall be put forward in future parliaments, may have good and gracious answer and remedy ordained before their departure from each parliament'. The petition began, however—as petitions often did—with a sort of preamble, which explained why the petition was being made: these explanatory preambles quite commonly began with the words 'Forasmuch as . . .' (*pur ce qe*).[18] The explanation given in this case[19] is that the Commons have had experience in previous parliaments of petitions and bills being left unanswered. And this is how they put it. They do not say: 'Forasmuch as common petitions and bills presented by the Commons in parliament have been left unanswered in times past . . .' What they do say is: 'Forasmuch as petitions and bills presented in parliament *by divers persons from among the Commons* ('par diverses persones des Communes') . . .' have been left unanswered in times past. That is a very revealing phrase: it reveals quite clearly that common petitions were in 1379 thought of as petitions presented '*by divers persons from among* the Commons', and not necessarily as petitions presented by the general body of the Commons in a corporate capacity.

Let us now look at a third and last document, this time one of the common petitions presented in the parliament of March 1348.[20] These 1348 petitions are all introduced by the words 'Item prie la Commune'. 'La Commune', whoever that may have been, but quite possibly it means 'the Commons', was evidently apprehensive that an attempt might be made in the parliament of March 1348 to change some of the answers that the King had made to petitions in the previous parliament, by petitioning against them. So 'la Commune' petitions that the King will not change those answers in response to any petition that may now be put forward. But the terms in which 'la Commune' made their

---

[18] e.g. ibid. iii.64(40).

[19] i.e. the case of the common petition of 1379.

[20] *Rot. Parl.* ii.203(30). See Appendix, p. 83.

request are interesting. 'La Commune' prays 'that the petitions presented by the said Commune in the last parliament, and fully answered and granted by the King and the Lords, may be upheld; and that the answers formerly given be not changed because of any bill presented in this parliament in the name of the Commune or of anyone else, for if any such bill going contrary [to those answers] be presented in parliament, "la Commune" does not avow it.' Here again, as in the statute of 1372, there is talk of somebody presenting 'in the name of the Commune' a petition which the 'Commune' disagrees with or will disagree with. And in 1348 here is that actual word 'avow' collocated with 'la Commune' on the one hand, and a petition, or at any rate a possible petition, on the other. This single word 'avow' has been enough to cause some historians[21] to take a flying leap to the conclusion that common petitions were in fact 'avowed' by the Commons acting in some sort of corporate capacity. But what does the petition in fact say? It does not say that 'La Commune' either does or does not 'avow' any petition *actually presented* in the name of the Commune: all it says is that 'La Commune' does not 'avow' such and such a petition *if it is presented* in the name of the Commune. But clearly 'La Commune' does not know whether such a petition has in fact been presented, and evidently can no more prevent its being presented 'in the name of the Commune' than the Commons in 1372 could prevent the lawyers who were knights of the shire from presenting petitions 'in the name of the Commons'.

Altogether, therefore, although the petitions called 'common petitions' or 'petitions of the Commons' ran 'in the name of the Commons' (as the statute of 1372 puts it) or 'in the name of the Commune' (as the 1348 petition expresses it), they were not (as some historians have wished to suppose) 'avowed' by the Commons as a body, by the Commons in a corporate capacity: rather they were thought of (as the petition of 1379 shows) as being presented by 'divers persons from among the Commons'. In other words, 'common petitions' did not possess their quality of 'commonness' because they were presented by the Commons as a body. They

---

[21] e.g. Stubbs, in *Constitutional History*, iii.478–9, a passage soundly criticized by D. Rayner, op. cit., especially pp. 199–206.

derived their quality of commonness partly indeed from the fact that they were presented by 'divers persons *from among the Commons*', i.e. by persons who were present in parliament in a representative capacity, but basically the common petitions derived their quality of commonness rather from the 'common people' to whom they purported to refer than from the 'Commons' by whom they purported to be presented. This view is borne out by the fact that when the Commons adopted—as they did rather later in our period—the procedure of putting forward petitions 'on behalf of' singular persons, such petitions were indeed duly enrolled in the parliament rolls, but they were not enrolled in the section that was set apart for 'common petitions'. So in the eyes of the chancery clerks who compiled the parliament rolls, a petition presented 'in the name of the Commons' was not necessarily and *ipso facto* a 'common petition'. The implications of that fact will become clearer if we turn our attention now from 'common petitions' to 'singular petitions'.

LECTURE 5

Petitions and Bills II

In the last lecture I began dealing with petitions and bills, and I spent most of the time discussing Common Petitions. There is a good deal more that might still be said about them, but we must now move on to the subject of Singular Petitions. This is the more necessary because Common Petitions have had a good deal of notice in writings on parliamentary history during the last half century or so,[1] whereas Singular Petitions have received, in comparison, rather less than their due share of attention; yet they too have played an important part in the development of parliament and of its manner of working.

We saw last time[2] that singular petitions were enrolled in great numbers on the parliament roll of 1305, but in very much smaller numbers on the parliament rolls of our period, though in growing numbers during its latter half. The reason for the much greater number of singular petitions enrolled on the parliament roll of 1305 is that the roll of 1305 enrols the whole corpus of singular petitions that were submitted and answered, whether the answer was given by the Triers, or by one or other of the courts to which the petition was referred by the Triers, or by the Chancellor, or by the King and his council in parliament. The reason for the much smaller number of singular petitions enrolled on the parliament rolls of our period is that our rolls record, not the whole corpus of singular petitions that were submitted and answered, but in the main only such singular petitions as needed to be answered 'by the King by authority of parliament', as the contemporary phrase often expressed it. What sorts of things did such petitions ask for?

One of the things which they frequently asked for arose out of a

[1] See especially the works referred to on p. 45, n. 3.
[2] See above, pp. 48–50.

development which was very characteristic of England in the fourteenth and fifteenth centuries. Starting with the troubles of Edward II's reign, England witnessed a series of political proscriptions which continued, at longer or shorter intervals, for the rest of the medieval period: the Despensers in 1320; Lancaster and the 'contrariants' in 1322; the Despensers again in 1327; in 1330 first Edmund, Earl of Kent, and then Roger Mortimer, Earl of March; the proscriptions of 1388 and the counter-proscriptions of 1397; the overthrow of Richard II in 1399; the risings of the Percys against Henry IV; and finally the proscriptions and counter-proscriptions of the period of the Wars of the Roses. These proscriptions mostly took the form of treason trials in parliament, and as condemnation for treason involved not only death for the condemned person, but also forfeiture and the 'corrupting' (as it was called) of his blood, these proscriptions affected the status of the descendants and heirs of the condemned person—unless something was done to re-habilitate them. Such rehabilitation—when the heat of a crisis had died down and circumstances had changed—was not infrequently achieved, sometimes even by the condemned persons themselves if they had managed by timely flight to escape execution, but more often by descendants or heirs. Such rehabilitations might not occur until after considerable lapses of time—thus some of the rehabilitations made in the reign of Richard II had reference to events in the reign of Edward II. As these various proscriptions had been staged in parliament, their legal effects could be undone only by parliament, and therefore the recognized procedure was for the person concerned to ask for rehabilitation by petitioning the King in parliament. *During the earlier half of our period*, a large proportion of the few singular petitions enrolled in the parliament rolls are petitions for rehabilitation of one sort or another. Several of them, incidentally, are more or less delayed repercussions of the proscriptions of 1327 and 1330. Take for instance the petition of John Matravers (or Maltravers) in the parliament of 1352,[3] twenty years after the event. Matravers had been an active partisan of Roger Mortimer in the 1320s and after Mortimer's fall had been condemned to death as a traitor for his alleged share in bringing

[3] *Rot. Parl.* ii.243–4(54–6).

about the death of Edmund, Earl of Kent, in 1330. But he had managed to escape to the continent. After the outbreak of the Hundred Years War, he was able to render some useful services to Edward III in Flanders, and the King rewarded him by granting him a charter of full restitution.[4] In the parliament of 1352, however, Matravers petitioned that this charter of restitution, which he described as having been granted 'by the King's royal power, with the common assent of prelates, earls, and barons of the realm', should now be 'renewed in this full parliament' i.e. the parliament of 1352. His petition was endorsed by the council and the lords with the words: 'It seems to the Council that, if it please the King, the Charter should be renewed and entered as of record on the roll of parliament.' The petition so endorsed was 'shown' to the King, who granted it, and apparently it was 'shown' also to the Commons, because the record in the parliament roll states, not only that the charter was 'granted' by the King, but that it was 'also granted by the "Commune" '. The new charter of restitution was expressly stated to be issued 'for the greater security of the status' of Matravers, and it was issued in the express terms that it was granted 'by assent of the prelates, dukes, earls, barons and commune of our realm of England *attending in our present parliament*'. ' "Common form" ', you say, 'words, words, words'. Not quite, I think—not mere words, anyway. We must not overlook one point when dealing with these petitions. Behind all of them there was probably a legal adviser; at any rate we must certainly never assume that these petitions were tossed off by the petitioners themselves.

In these petitions we are meeting, not the petitioner alone, but the petitioner *and his legal adviser*. The legal adviser who presumably drafted the petition which Matravers presented in the parliament of 1352 evidently took the view that a charter renewed by the King 'in full parliament' would be stronger in law than the previous charter issued by the King 'by his royal power'— for although that previous charter had been issued by the King 'with the common assent of the prelates, earls, and barons of the

[4] *The Dictionary of National Biography* vol. XII, pp. 891–2; *The Complete Peerage*, vol. VIII, pp. 581–6.

realm', that assent had not been described as having been given 'in full parliament'. The new charter contained the express statement that it was granted 'by assent of the prelates, dukes, earls, barons and Commune of our realm of England *attending in our present parliament*'. In other words, Matravers had been advised by his lawyer that if he wanted the greatest possible legal security for his status—and the greatest possible legal security for his status was what everybody would want when he was being rehabilitated after the dangerous experience of being condemned as a traitor— he must get from the King, not a charter granted 'by royal power', but a charter granted by assent, by authority, of parliament.

I have dwelt a little on this question of rehabilitation, partly because it is one of the things that these (enrolled) singular petitions often ask for during our period, and partly also because it gives a general clue to the purport of these enrolled singular petitions as a whole. Their purport is too various, I think, to be *defined*, but it can be *described* in very general terms as being 'to get the law altered in favour of the petitioner', on the ground that his is a hard case, or a special case, a hard case or special case which cannot be met by judicial action, but requires a remedy which has a touch of what we would call 'legislative' quality about it. One of the simplest examples of this is provided by a series of singular petitions enrolled for the most part in the parliament rolls of Henry V's reign. Because of the rising of Owain Glyndwr in Wales, a statute was made in the parliament of 1401 disabling men of Welsh birth from buying lands or tenements in England, or in the boroughs and English towns within Wales.[5] Now this statute would obviously bear hardly upon men of Welsh birth who were resident in England and who had taken no part in Glyndwr's rising. A series of such persons successfully petitioned the King to be exempted 'by authority of parliament' from the operations of the statute. Thus in the parliament roll of 1414, for example, there are three such petitions enrolled consecutively:[6] one of the petitioners[7] describes himself as a freeman of the city of London,

---

[5] *Rot. Parl.* iii.472–3(77); *Statutes of the Realm*, ii.129 (2 Hen. IV, c. 20).

[6] *Rot. Parl.* iv.44–5(27,28,29).

[7] Lewis John.

and the other two[8] describe themselves as 'esquires'. (It seems quite likely, by the way, that the three employed the same legal adviser, for their petitions are in all material respects verbally identical.)

Now these 'singular petitions' or 'particular bills' enrolled in the parliament rolls of our period were the origin of what came to be known in the sixteenth century and later as 'private bills'—as distinct from 'public bills', the public bills being of general application, the 'private bills' being concerned with personal or sectional interests. By the second half of the sixteenth century—as Sir John Neale has emphasized in his book on the Elizabethan House of Commons[9]—'private bills' were taking up a great deal of parliament's time, and were being promoted not only by singular persons in the literal sense, but also by local bodies like the boroughs, and especially by the gilds and companies of the city of London. In the eighteenth century these 'private bills' were used in great numbers to authorize enclosures and the construction of canals, and in the nineteenth century they were used in still greater numbers to authorize the construction of railways. So 'private bills' became an extremely important branch of parliamentary activity, and though they are not now anything like as numerous as they were, they are still in use. From our point of view, however, their importance in the sixteenth and later centuries is only prospective, something that is still to come. Have they any interest for us who are concerned with the second century of the English parliament, rather than with its fourth, or fifth, or sixth century? I believe they have a very considerable interest from the standpoint of the development of parliament and its procedure.

We have seen[10] that during the first half of our period, 'singular petitions' were handed in to the Receivers who were appointed at the beginning of each parliament, and then were sorted and sent on by them to be answered by the Triers or Auditors of Petitions, who might, however, send some of them on to be answered by

[8] John Montgomery and John Stiward.
[9] J. E. Neale, *The Elizabethan House of Commons* (London, 1949), p. 383.
[10] See above, pp. 47-8.

the King and his council if the nature of the request was such that the King had to be consulted. The singular petitions enrolled on the parliament rolls during the earlier half of our period were all petitions that had been sent forward in this way by the Triers. Then, just about the middle of our period—round about 1400— we find that the singular petitions enrolled in the parliament rolls are being channelled, so to speak, in two streams. On the one hand is the long-established channel through the Receivers to the Triers, and from the Triers to the King and his council in parliament if the singular petition made a request that needed to be answered by the King by authority of parliament. The singular petitions in this long-established channel are in the traditional form, i.e. the petitioner addresses his petition directly to the King—the King alone, or the King and his council, or the King and the Lords. On the other hand is the new channel: the singular petitions in this stream are in a form which is in one respect very new and also very significant. In this stream, the petitioner addresses his petition not to the King (either alone, or together with his council, or together with the Lords)—not to the King, but to '*the Commons in parliament*'.[11] And what 'the Commons in parliament' are requested by the petitioner to do is always the same thing. After explaining the circumstances and the difficulty in which he finds himself, the petitioner asks 'the Commons in parliament' to make a 'request' to the King that he will 'ordain by authority of parliament' the remedy which the petitioner specifies in his petition. In other words, 'the Commons in parliament' are asked to act as inter-mediaries between the singular person and the King—in fact a petitioner sometimes actually employs the medieval English word for an intermediary, the word 'mean', and speaks of 'the Commons in parliament' as being a 'mean' between himself and the King.[12] Notice that 'the Commons in parliament' are *not* asked by the petitioner to ordain the remedy: the petitioner is always explicit that the remedy must be ordained by the King 'by authority of parliament'. All that the Commons are asked by the petitioner to

[11] Cf. A. R. Myers, art. cit., *E.H.R.*, LII (1937), pp. 398–404. See Appendix, D(i), pp. 84–7.

[12] Cf. Appendix, D(i), pp. 86–7, under 1421.

do is to request the King to ordain 'by authority of parliament' the remedy which the petitioner specifies.[13] If the Commons comply with what the petitioner asked them to do, then his petition will reach the King incapsulated in a petition of the Commons requesting the King to do what the petitioner asks. But this 'covering petition' (if I may so term it) of the Commons was not regarded as a 'common petition' in the technical sense that I was discussing last time. These 'covering petitions' of the Commons are not entered in the parliament rolls in the section set apart for 'Common Petitions'. They are entered on the roll by the clerk one by one, each with such a preface as, for example, this one:

'Item, a petition was handed in by the Commons in parliament for Sir Walter Hungerford in the form that follows:' and then the text of the petition is transcribed.[14] Opposite the entry, the clerk then writes in the margin 'For Sir Walter Hungerford'. Now the form in which these petitions are entered on the parliament roll is significant: 'a petition was handed in by the Commons in parliament for Sir Walter Hungerford'. In other words, although the petition is handed in by the Commons, and is in that sense a petition *of* the Commons, nevertheless it is not classified as a 'common petition' in the technical sense, precisely because it is 'for Sir Walter Hungerford'. As it is '*for* Sir Walter Hungerford' it 'touches' not 'common people' but a 'singular person', and therefore it is not classified as a common petition. 'More technicalities', you say. So what?

I said at the beginning of this present lecture that common petitions have had a good deal of notice in writings on parliamentary history, whereas singular petitions have in comparison received rather less than their due share of attention—'rather less than their due share' because they too have played quite an important part in the development of parliament and of its manner of working. I would like now to try to develop that point.

Common petitions are so numerous—as I have said before,

13 Such petitions are clearly referred to as a class in 1425 (*Rot. Parl.* iv.301(21)). See Appendix, D(ii), p. 87.

14 *Rot. Parl.* iii.632(40). Hungerford's petition, handed in by the Commons, dates from 1410. See Appendix, D(i), p. 86.

there are some two thousand of them enrolled in the parliament rolls of the hundred years or so with which we are concerned—that their mere bulk makes them the most obvious feature of the parliament rolls, at any rate from about the beginning of our period to the end of the Middle Ages. Moreover, the fact that these common petitions are known to have formed the ground-work, and even provided the basic drafts, of many of the very numerous statutes enrolled in the bulky medieval Statute Rolls, this fact has still further—and quite rightly—enhanced their significance in the eyes of historians. And common petitions do explain so many things in Parliament. For instance, they provide the his-torical explanation of the fact that in later times bills passed by the Commons could not become law until they had been submitted first to the Lords, who possessed and exercised the power of amendment and of outright rejection, and then ultimately to the King, who also possessed and exercised the power of refusing his assent. The historical explanation of all this is quite clearly supplied by the medieval procedure of the common petitions. The ex-planation is indeed clear, very clear—so far as it goes. But it doesn't go far enough. In fact, it only goes half-way.

The procedure of parliamentary law-making was not a one-way traffic, but a two-way traffic. There were not merely the bills going up from the Commons to the Lords, the Lords having the power to accept or reject or amend the bills that were sent up to them. There were also the bills going down from the Lords to the Com-mons, the Commons having the power to accept or reject or amend the bills that were sent down to them. That two-way traffic was certainly in existence by the end of our period, though not, I think, at the beginning of it. Now the medieval procedure of common petitions provides the historical explanation only of the traffic of bills from the Commons to the Lords: it does not supply any historical explanation of the traffic *from the Lords to the Commons*. It is perhaps fair to add that nobody has argued that the procedure of common petitions does supply an historical ex-planation of the traffic from the Lords to the Commons: they have just ignored the difficulty. But the difficulty is there all the same. When the Commons sent their bills to the Lords, historically they were petitioners. But when the Commons received the bills of the Lords, it was not—it could not be—in the capacity of petitioners that they received them. How then did the two-way traffic begin? How—*not* why—at any rate for the present—did the Lords come to send bills to the Commons? Let us turn again to the singular petitions which I was discussing a few minutes ago.

We saw that at about the middle of our period, there were two streams of these singular petitions, (i) the historically older stream, in which the petitioner addressed his petition directly to the King; and (ii) the historically new stream, in which the petitioner addressed his petition to 'the Commons in parliament', asking them to be intermediaries between him and the King, and to request the King to grant his petition 'by authority of parliament'.

Presumably the petitions of the older stream, which were addressed directly to the King, were handed to the Receivers, who passed them to the Triers, who passed them on to the King and his council in parliament. The petitions of the new stream, which were addressed to the Commons, may also have been passed on by the Commons through the Receivers and Triers, but the Commons would be more likely, I would have thought, to hand them to the Clerk of the Parliament, as they did with the common petitions, and the Clerk would then pass them to the King and his council. Indeed, it is possible that one reason for devising the new form of singular petition addressed to the Commons may have been that the legal advisers of the petitioners thought that a petition passed by the Commons through the Clerk of the Parliament would get to the King and his council more directly and quickly than if passed through the Receivers and the Triers. However, by whatever route they went, the singular petitions of both streams eventually reached the King and his council in parliament.

Now the singular petitions of the *new* stream, being addressed to the Commons, could only reach the King and his council if the Commons agreed to send them on. So the fact that they had reached the King meant that they came with the assent of the Commons behind them. If the King and the Lords now agreed to them they were enacted in a formula which after a short period of variations eventually took a form to the effect that the petition was granted by the King with the advice and assent of the Lords and at the request of the Commons. There were occasional variations in the wording, but King, Lords, and Commons were all brought into the enacting clause in one way or another—'with the assent' *or* 'with the advice and assent of the Lords'; 'at the request of the Commons' at first, but later 'with the assent of the Commons'.

How about the singular petitions of the older stream—those which were addressed directly to the King? We find that these are also granted by the same enacting formulas as the new-style petitions—formulas which state that they are enacted, not only with the advice and assent of the Lords, but also 'at the request' or later 'with the assent' of the Commons.[15] Now the words 'at the request of the Commons' in the enacting clause of the *new* form of petition mean exactly what they say, because the new form of petition was addressed to the Commons, and only went forward to the King if the Commons submitted it as intermediaries. What does the phrase mean in the enacting clause of the *old* petitions, which were addressed directly to the King or to the King and the Lords? There is no time here to go into the details of the evidence, but taken together it indicates quite clearly that these singular petitions of the older style, although not addressed to the Commons, were increasingly being sent, by Henry V's reign, not merely to the King and Lords to whom they were addressed, but also to the Commons for their 'assent' or supporting 'request'. This seems to be the historical beginning of the two-way traffic in bills between Lords and Commons, though in some senses the way for this development had been prepared by the procedure of the subsidy-indentures. By the end of our period that two-way traffic was in essentials established not only in subsidy-indentures, and not only in private bills, but also in common petitions and bills as well. The establishing of that two-way traffic in bills of all kinds is the first of the really big developments to occur in the English parliament subsequent to its transformation into a parliament that was representative.

---

[15] The Welsh petitions of 1414 (*Rot. Parl.* iv.44–5) are examples.

The Commons in their 'Common House'

In all the preceding lectures we have been concerned with parliament as a whole. In this final lecture I would like to look more particularly at the Commons. Already, in connection both with taxation and with petitions, we have been very much aware of the *existence* of the Commons, but we have been looking at them mainly in the context, so to speak, of the Parliament Chamber, when they met the King and his council and the Lords in the White Chamber. This time I propose that we look at them rather in the context of their own meeting-place—the Painted Chamber, the Chapter House, or the Refectory, as the case may be—what the parliament rolls of the fifteenth century usually refer to as their 'Common House'.

Now during our period it is true to say that in a broad sense all the meetings of the Commons in their 'Common House' were preparatory. As we have seen, the 'charge' often propounded questions to which the Commons had—as John of Gaunt expressed it in 1376—'to make an answer', and during our period the commonest, most commonly recurring, of these questions was the question of taxation. Again, as we have also seen, the 'charge' invited petitions, both 'singular' petitions and 'common' petitions. It was in the discussions in the 'Common House' that the Commons reached their 'answers' to the questions propounded to them, and presumably expressed any common assent that might be given to any common petition. All this was 'preparatory'—preparatory to 'making' the answers and 'putting forward' the petitions. And in one sense, these preparatory discussions are the biggest of all the historical problems concerning the Commons in their Common House. (Notice, by the way, that I say 'discussions'. The books usually say 'debates', but personally I think that the term 'debates' inevitably suggests to our modern minds all sorts of things which may mislead us, and mislead us the more dangerously because they mislead us unconsciously. For our purpose it is better to avoid the 'coloured' word 'debates', and stick to the 'grey' word 'discussions'.)

Now the making of 'answers' necessarily involved a certain amount of organization, and we have already noticed in passing what that organization was. We have seen that 'answers' were made by a delegation which went on behalf of the whole body of the Commons to the King and the Lords in the White Chamber. But that was not all the organization that was called for. The making of answers—especially to questions about taxation—involved prior conferences between the delegates of the Commons and delegates of the Lords. The Commons seem to have employed the same delegates for both purposes, both for making answers and for conferences, but the Lords had to produce a delegation *ad hoc* for the conferences. Even the two delegations did not provide all the organization that was required. When the Commons' delegates appeared before the King and Lords in the White Chamber to make the 'answers', their answers were more often oral than written. This meant that the actual speaking had to be done by some individual among the delegates. And there, as everyone knows, you have the beginnings of the functionary known later as the Speaker, with a capital *S*.

The putting forward of common petitions, however, did not necessarily involve anything like as much organization as the making of 'answers'. We have seen that common petitions were 'put forward' by handing them to the Clerk of the Parliament. We have also seen[1] that common petitions could be described in the parliament roll of 1379 as being 'presented . . . by divers persons from among the Commons'.[2] Such petitions could be handed in to the Clerk of the Parliament by the 'divers persons' who promoted them with very little organization. If, on the other hand, some common petitions were considered and approved by the Commons as a body, then clearly a greater amount of organization

---

[1] See above, p. 53.
[2] *Rot. Parl.* iii.61(28).

would be necessary for dealing with them than for dealing with common petitions put forward by 'divers persons from among the Commons'.

It is obvious that the main clue to the historical problem of the Commons' 'discussions' in their 'Common House' is the earlier history of the office of Speaker. You will not expect me to tackle that dark and difficult subject in a single lecture.[3] But perhaps I may just touch on one or two of the matters that concern us here now.

As everyone knows, the Speaker in later times—I mean in times later than our period—has had a two-sided function. On the one hand, there is the function which was evidently his original function historically—the function of speaking on behalf of the delegation of the Commons in the Parliament Chamber in the presence of the King and the Lords. On the other hand, there is the function of presiding over the discussions and debates of the Commons in their 'Common House'. And historically this is the darkest aspect of the whole dark problem.

The root trouble is, of course, that there is no mention of anyone either bearing the title or performing any of the functions of a Speaker before 1343 or between 1343 and 1376, and it is not certain that the earliest person mentioned as performing the function—Sir William Trussell in 1343—was even one of the representatives in parliament. (On the other hand, it is not possible to accept the categorical assertion often made [4]that he definitely was not one of the representatives. He could have been knight of the shire, for instance, for Leicestershire, which seems to have been his home county.) For my own part I would be inclined to suppose that the function of speaking for the Commons' delegations in the Parliament Chamber may well have been performed during the dark period 1343 to 1376 by any member of the delegation as seemed most convenient on each occasion. There are one or two slight indications which seem to point to that supposition.

---

[3] At this point in his lecture as delivered, Sir Goronwy referred to the 'reliable promise of a book on the subject', i.e. J. S. Roskell, *The Commons and their Speakers 1376–1523* (Manchester, 1965).

[4] e.g. in Richardson and Sayles, *B.I.H.R.*, vol. IX (1931–2), p. 14, n. 6.

(a) When the office of Speaker was clearly established, as it was by the 1390s, the routine procedure was that the Speaker made his protestation[5]—what is nowadays misleadingly called 'asking for liberty of speech'—when presented to the King at the very beginning of the parliament. In the first half-dozen parliaments which we get after 1376, however, the parliament rolls record the Speaker as making his protestation, not at the very beginning of parliament, but when he first had occasion to appear in the Parliament Chamber to make an 'answer'. Another possibly significant fact is that in the parliament of November 1381, the Speaker's protestation, having been originally made on 18 November,[6] seems to have been repeated several days later when the Commons came into parliament to make an oral request.[7] But the most remarkable instance of that sort of thing was in the parliament of 1406, when the Speaker made his protestation at least *seven* times.[8] These various episodes, taken together, suggest that protestations were made on more occasions than are recorded, and that originally the spokesman of the Commons may have made a protestation on each occasion when they appeared to make an answer: which suggests that more than one man may have acted on the different occasions during each parliament.

(b) That possibility is suggested also by the account in the *Anonimalle Chronicle* of the parliament of 1376. The chronicle says[9] that on the first appearance of the Commons in the White Chamber, the Duke of Lancaster asked which of them was to do the speaking ('Quel de vous avera la parlaunce et pronunciation de ce qe vous avez ordine parentre vous?') And Peter de la Mare said it was he. When they appeared for a second time a few days later, the Duke again began the proceedings with the question 'Qi parlera?' And Peter de la Mare answered, 'As I told you three days

---

[5] For the Speaker's protestation, see Roskell, op. cit., especially chapter 2.

[6] *Rot. Parl.* iii.100(10).

[7] Ibid. 100(17).

[8] Ibid. 568(11), 569(13), 572(30), 573(34), 574(38), 577(41), 579(55). Presumably, when Tiptoft was presented by the Commons as their Speaker-elect, he made, as was then customary, his first protestation. That protestation, however, happens not to have been recorded in the parliament roll.

[9] *The Anonimalle Chronicle*, p. 83.

ago, sir, it has been ordained by common assent that I do the speaking on this occasion'.[10] It rather looks as if the Duke's opening 'Qi parlera?' was an established formula, a formula which presupposed that the man who did the speaking on the second occasion would not necessarily be the same man as had done it on the previous occasion.

(c) Another tiny straw which may be significant is this. In 1407, the King stated in parliament that the customary procedure was for the report of the taxes granted to the King 'by the Commons with the assent of the Lords' to be made by the Speaker of the Commons.[11] That procedure seems to have gone back to 1380 at any rate, for in the parliament of November 1380 the grant is recorded in the parliament roll as being reported by the Speaker of the Commons.[12] But in the parliaments of 1365, 1368, and 1372, the grants made in those parliaments are recorded as having been reported by the Chancellor in 1365 and 1372, and by the Archbishop of Canterbury in 1368.[13] Now the Commons were as active and important in the granting of taxes in the 1360s and 1370s as they were in the 1380s. The fact that their speaker did not then make the report may well have been because at that time there was no Speaker with a capital S, in other words that the Commons had only a spokesman with a small s, who might be any one of the Commons' delegation according to the necessities of the occasion.

I think therefore that before 1376 the speaking for the Commons' delegation may well have been done, not by a definitely constituted Speaker with a capital S, but by perhaps a shifting series of spokesmen with a small s. If so, it seems a reasonable supposition that these spokesmen would not, in virtue of being spokesmen, have any presidential duties.[14] On the other hand, it is hard to envisage discussions making much headway in a body of the number of the Commons, unless some guidance came from somewhere. The most likely source of such guidance, I would think, would be the delegation who were chosen to go to the

[10] Ibid., p. 85.   [11] *Rot. Parl.* iii.611(21).
[12] Ibid. 90(16).   [13] Ibid. ii.288(31), 310(12), 297(20).
[14] For a discussion of the problem of such 'duties', see Roskell, op. cit., chapter 4.

conference with the lords and then to the White Chamber to 'make answer'. Certainly in regard to the crucial matter of taxation, the delegates of the Commons, having already discussed the matter with the lords, would be the best qualified to give a lead to the discussion by the Commons. The account that we have in the parliament roll of the lengthy discussions that preceded the granting of the poll tax of 1380[15] suggests that the Commons' delegates played a formative part in attaining the grant that was ultimately made on that occasion.

Another point of considerable interest about the Commons' 'discussions' is—how did the Commons in their Common House bring their discussions to a decision? This is a question of interest, not merely from the point of view of seeing how the machine worked, but also from the point of view of understanding the legal and constitutional ideas which lay behind the machine.

There are repeated indications on several occasions in the parliament rolls[16] that the Lords in parliament reached their decisions 'severally' as the rolls put it, i.e. each lord gave his voice or vote in turn. The Lords however were summoned to parliament by the King as individuals, 'to treat with us and the magnates . . . and to give your counsel.' Moreover their numbers were not large, and it was therefore practicable to take their voices 'severally'. The Commons, on the other hand, were a much larger body, they were not summoned individually but as representatives of local communities, and legally they were summoned not to 'treat and give counsel' but to 'do and consent to those things which shall be ordained by common counsel of our kingdom'. As might therefore be expected, the Commons did not give their voices 'severally' like the Lords. How then did they give their 'voices'? This question evidently puzzled Stubbs. Speaking of the Commons he said, 'No authentic record has yet been found of the way in in which the general assent of the assembly was taken, or the result of a division ascertained. We might infer from the procuratorial character of the powers of the representatives that on some

[15] *Rot. Parl.* iii.89–90(12,13).
[16] Ibid. ii.139(19), 290(13), 295(7): iii.137(23), 426(73), 611(21).

questions, taxation in particular, the two members for each community would have only a joint vote.' He summarizes his whole paragraph in the marginal caption 'No light as yet on the method of voting'.[17]

Let us for a moment take a circuit and inquire what happened in later years. Let us begin as late as possible. In 1961[18], voting in the House of Commons takes two forms—voting by voices and voting by division. On every occasion, voting in the first instance always takes the form of voting by voices. That is, the Speaker says, 'Those in favour say "Aye", those against say "No"', and then the members shout. Voting by division, on the other hand, does not necessarily take place on every occasion, but only when the House so desires, and if it does take place at all, it can only occur *subsequent to* and *as a supplement to* the voting by voices. When voting by division does take place, the 'Ayes' go into one lobby, and the 'Noes' into the other lobby.

Round about 1565 Sir Thomas Smith described the procedure of parliament as it then was in his book *De Republica Anglorum*. Here is just his account of the voting in the House of Commons of his day: '. . . . the speaker asketh if they will goe to the question. And if they agree, he holdeth the bill up in his hande and sayeth, As many as will have this bill goe forwarde . . . say Yea. Then they which allowe the bill crie Yea, and as many as will not, say No: as the crie of Yea or No is bigger, so the bill is allowed or dashed. If it be a doubt which crie is the bigger, they divide the house, the speaker saying, As many as doe allowe the bill, goe downe with the bill, and as many as do not, sitte still. So they divide themselves, and being so divided they are numbred who make the more part, and so the bill doeth speede.'[19] (As you see, the only material difference between the voting procedure of the Commons in 1961 and in 1565 is that in the divisions of 1961 both 'Ayes' and 'Noes' go out, each into a separate lobby, and are then counted, whereas

[17] *Constitutional History*, ii. 265–6. Stubbs's mention of 'the procuratorial character of the powers of the representatives' is a reference to the full powers which each pair of representatives had from the shire or borough they represented.

[18] The year these Lectures were delivered.

[19] Sir Thomas Smith, *De Republica Anglorum*, ed. L. Alston (Cambridge, 1906), p. 56.

in 1565 only the 'Ayes' went out of the chamber, and the 'Noes' sat still.)

For our present purpose, the significant point to notice is this: in the House of Commons, votes are *counted* only when there is voting by division. When the voting is by voices, everybody votes simultaneously by shouting 'Aye' or 'No', and the Speaker decides which is the majority according (in Smith's words in 1565) 'as the *crie* of Yea or No is *bigger*'. In other words, when voting in the House of Commons, whether in 1961 or in 1565, is by voices, the majority is revealed, not by counting but by hearing, not by numbers but by sound. 'Too fanciful a way of putting it', you say, 'too fanciful altogether.' That remains to be seen!

In 1555, in other words ten years before Smith's *De Republica Anglorum*, there was a case taken before the Court of Common Pleas. Of the four judges on the bench, two were among the greatest lawyers of the sixteenth century, Sir Robert Brooke, the Chief Justice of Common Pleas, and Sir William Staunford, both still revered by English common lawyers. Incidentally, all four judges had each already been three times elected to the House of Commons, and the Chief Justice had actually been Speaker of the Commons in the parliament of the previous year. Incidentally, also, the case was reported by the great Edmund Plowden in his *Commentaries*,[20] which is one of the big books of the English common lawyers. Plowden evidently thought that the case was of interest from the legal point of view. The case was the case of Buckley *versus* Thomas.[21]

In September 1553 there had been a contested election in Anglesey. Welsh counties, by the provisions of the so-called Act of Union of 1536, had only one representative in parliament, not two like the English shires. For the single Anglesey seat two

[20] *Les Commentaries ou Reports de Edmund Plowden* (1684 edn.), pp. 118–31, translated in *Commentaries or Reports of Edmund Plowden* (1779 edn.), pp. 118–31.

[21] This case was again, although more briefly, discussed by Sir Goronwy in his Presidential Addresses to the Royal Historical Society of December 1963 and 1964: 'The Emergence of Majority Rule in English Parliamentary Elections', *Transactions of the Royal Historical Society*, 5th series, vol. 14 (on pp. 187–91) and 'The Emergence of Majority Rule in the Procedure of the House of Commons', ibid., 5th series, vol. 15 (p. 167, n. 2).

names had been proposed to the electors in 1553—Sir Richard
Buckley and William Lewis. The sheriff, Rice Thomas, returned
William Lewis as having been elected. Buckley maintained that it
was he and not Lewis that had in reality been chosen by the
majority of the electors, and if this was so, then the sheriff had been
guilty of making an undue return. A statute of 1445[22] had
prescribed that a sheriff who made an undue return should forfeit
a penalty of £100 to the aggrieved person. Sir Richard Buckley
accordingly brought an action against the sheriff to recover the
£100 penalty, and that was how the matter came up before the
Court of Common Pleas in 1555.

A number of preliminary legal points were put forward. One of
the legal arguments put forward by the counsel for the defendant
sheriff was that Buckley's statement that he had been elected by a
majority was not legally acceptable, because he had not, as counsel
put it, 'shown the certainty of the number', i.e. had not stated the
number who had voted for him and the number who had voted
for Lewis. The four judges who took the case all rejected this
submission, and in doing so made some remarks about majorities
—majorities in parliamentary elections—which are nevertheless
very relevant to our present purpose, and which are all the more
interesting because it happened (as I have said) that all four judges
had each already been three times elected to the House of Commons, and one of them had actually been Speaker of the Commons: so they were not merely learned in the law, but also had
personal experience of parliament.

Mr. Justice Staunford, who gave his judgment first said:[23] 'It
seems to me that the plaintiff shall not be compelled to show the
certain number of the electors, for since he cannot be intended to
have certain knowledge thereof, he shall not therefore be compelled to show the certainty. And perhaps he was elected by voices
or by holding up of hands, and not by the number of persons in
certain, in which case it is easy to determine who hath the majority
of voices or hands by hearing or seeing, and yet very difficult to
know the certain number of the names of them.' It would suffice

[22] *Statutes of the Realm*, ii.340–42 (23 Hen. VI, c. 14).
[23] *Les Commentaries*, p. 123.

therefore, Staunford stated, that the plaintiff 'shall say generally that he was elected by the greater number'. Notice these words 'generally . . . by the greater number', i.e. by the majority but without knowing or stating specifically what the majority was. The same point was made by the Chief Justice, Sir Robert Brooke,[24] who having remarked that he had himself been elected in London by holding up of hands but could not tell *how many* there were that held up their hands, concluded with these words: 'So if the election [in Anglesey] was in any such manner (as we have no reason to take it otherwise), the plaintiff could not possibly be intended to know the certain number of the electors. And to put him to disclose a certainty where he cannot by any possibility be presumed to know or remember the certainty is not reasonable, nor requisite in our law . . .'. A third judge, Mr. Justice Saunders, had made the same point.[25] And the fourth judge concurred in everything.

It is evident from what the judges said on this occasion that in the Anglesey election of 1553 there had not been a poll, i.e. that the voters had not been individually counted, for if there had been a poll, the number who had voted for each candidate would have been known. Now by the eighteenth century it seems to have been usual, if there was a contest, to take the proceedings right through to a poll—unless, of course, as did happen from time to time, a sufficient number of candidates 'declined the poll', as the phrase went, i.e. withdrew from the contest, and therefore in effect left the election uncontested. But whatever may have become usual by the eighteenth century, what these judges said in 1555 shows that in the sixteenth century a contested election was not necessarily taken to a poll but could be determined—as Staunford put it—'by voices or by holding up of hands, and not by the number of persons in certain . . . by hearing or seeing . . .'[26] In other words, the 'greater number' in parliamentary elections was not necessarily, in the eyes of the law, something that was counted: it was

[24] Ibid. p. 128.
[25] Ibid., p. 126.
[26] Election by voices in Elizabeth I's reign has been described by J. E. Neale (op. cit., pp. 86–8).

something that might also be recognized 'by hearing or seeing'. 'Fanciful', do you still say? 'Fanciful' in the Court of Common Pleas? ('Tell me, where is Fancy bred?') 'Well, anyway', you say, 'that may be the law about majorities *in parliamentary elections*, but we didn't notice that these learned judges said anything about majorities *in divisions in the House of Commons*, which is the point we started from'. I was just coming to that. One of these four judges, Sir Edwin Saunders, did in fact refer to the subject of majorities in parliament.

In order, in his judgment, to illustrate the difference between an electoral majority 'by voices or hands' and a majority known by counting, Saunders takes an example from parliament, and as he had already served as a member of the House of Commons three times—in 1541, in 1547, and as recently as 1553—he was in a good position to know what he was talking about. 'In parliament', he says, 'the majority of voices in the Upper House may be easily known, because they are demanded severally, and the Clerk of the House reckons them; but in the Lower House of parliament it is otherwise, *for there the assent is tried by the voices sounding all at one time*, and therefore if the assent there were issuable [i.e. at issue], the party should say, generally by the greater number . . . and so likewise in the case here'.[27]

Now those remarks of Saunders's, though naturally more brief than Sir Thomas Smith's description ten years later, are almost more significant for our present purpose. According to Saunders, the majority principle was indeed operative in both Houses of Parliament, but whereas in the Lords it was a majority revealed by counting, in the Commons it was a majority revealed by sound. In other words, Saunders is saying that at the time when he was giving his judgment, in 1555, the Commons did not vote by dividing, but by voices. Ten years later, Sir Thomas Smith says that if there was 'doubt which crie is the bigger, they divide the house': in other words Smith treats voting by division as an established procedure of the Commons in 1565. But he does not say whether at that time it was a procedure that was often resorted to. The evidence of the Journals of the House, however,

[27] *Les Commentaries*, p. 126.

indicates pretty clearly that divisions were relatively few until the very last years of the sixteenth century. You will remember that Sir John Neale has said[28] that 'if the Commons Journals can be trusted, divisions were rare before Elizabeth's reign'—only seven divisions, he finds, in all nine sessions of the reigns of Edward VI and Mary. The remarks of Mr. Justice Saunders in 1555 indicate that on this point the Commons Journals *can* be trusted: Saunders may not have been literally accurate in implying that voting in the House of Commons was *always* by voices in 1555, but his emphasis was right: in the House of Lords in 1555 the 'greater number' was already being identified by counting—'the Clerk of the House *reckons* them', he says; but in the House of Commons, the 'greater number' (almost always) was still not something that was *counted*, but something that was *heard*. From the historian's point of view, therefore, what Saunders says in 1555 is a flash of evidence which by good luck lights up the slow process of transition at a very significant moment, at the very moment when the Commons were about to recognize that the 'greater number' might some-times have to be counted. During Elizabeth's reign, as Sir John Neale has shown,[29] voting by divisions very gradually became relatively more frequent; but only very gradually, and in a fashion which indicates that even yet the Commons were not saying plainly—or thinking plainly—that a vote carried by a majority of one is every whit as effectual as a unanimous vote! They seem indeed to have had a curious sort of *arrière pensée* about a majority achieved by dividing. And they indicated it by their procedure.

If a bill was carried by a majority by voices, that was that. But if a bill was carried by a majority by dividing, that was *not* that! Further procedure followed. The standing order was that when a bill was carried by a majority on a division, then all the members of the House present, as well those who had voted against it as those who had voted for it, went out of the chamber taking the bill with them, and then came back into the chamber and presented the bill to the Speaker, saying that they 'warranted' it.[30]

Now the historian would give a great deal to know when and

28 Op. cit., p. 399.   29 Op. cit., pp. 398, 399.   30 Neale, op. cit., pp. 397–8.

by whom that grave pantomime was devised and introduced. In Elizabethan times it was spoken of as an 'ancient order',[31] but as it occurred only when a bill was carried *on a division*, manifestly it is unlikely to have been older than divisions, and, as we have seen, divisions in the House of Commons were still very rare as late as 1555. Sir John Neale has observed[32] that this procedure 'clearly had its origin in the twin medieval ideas that law-making involved the consent of the whole community and that members were attorneys for their constituencies'. That is certainly true, but it can hardly be the whole truth, because it does not explain why the procedure was followed only after a division. Why was it not followed also when the voting had been by voices, for voices could—and did—cry 'No' as well as 'Aye'. Why had a majority by division to be 'warranted', whereas a majority by voices had not? Presumably because a majority by division was in some significant way different from a majority by voices. In what way?

We have already seen that one manifest difference was that a majority by division was counted, whereas a majority by voices was heard, that a majority by division was a majority by a specific number, whereas a majority by voices was—as Saunders in 1555 had put it[33]—'*generally*, by the greater number'. When they proceeded from voices to a division, majority was plucked out of the happy haze of generality, and flung into the cold light of enumeration. While they stuck to voices, they cried 'Aye', 'No' pell-mell, yet they all stayed together in one chamber. But when they divided, they no longer stayed together—the 'Ayes' went forth, the 'Noes' sat still.[34] It is significant that in the pantomime of warranting the bill, the 'Ayes' and the 'Noes' all went forth together, and then returned into the chamber together.[35] It was not a 'substantive vote'—'Ayes' remained 'Ayes' and 'Noes' remained 'Noes', but the ceremony did indicate at any rate a common will that the majority decision should be accepted as the common counsel. But that still did not quite go without saying—so they said it in dumb show.

We have had to take rather a circuit, but now at length we are

[31] Ibid., p. 397.   [32] Ibid., p. 398.   [33] See above, p. 75.
[34] Neale, op. cit., p. 397.   [35] Ibid.

back to where we started—Stubb's marginal summary,[36] 'No light as yet on the method of voting'. There can be little doubt, I think, that the method used by the Commons during our period was the method of voting by voices, which continued to be their only method until about the middle of the sixteenth century, when voting by division came in as a supplement to, but never as a substitute for, voting by voices.

So I don't think that Englishmen ever until the (late) nineteenth century said 'plainly that', as Maitland put it,[37] 'a vote carried by a majority of one is for certain purposes every whit as effectual as a unanimous vote'. What they did say, I think, was that *common* assent was for certain purposes every whit as effectual as *unanimous* assent; in fact more effectual, in the sense that common assent was always attainable while unanimous assent was often not attainable, and majority assent was the clue to, the index to, the key to, the common assent. 'There is fiction there: [but] not fiction if that term means falsehood'.[38] It was because 'the majority' was not a precise term that the *heard* majority of 'voices' was a good index to the *common* view. Note what Maitland also said:[39] '*Common . . .* is the word which haunts us in the middle ages. . . . All is common; nothing public . . .'. That passage might be adapted—'they [the Commons] were chosen by common election of communities to parliament and in the Commons' House do and consent to what should be ordained by *common* counsel'. 'All is *common*'— the *common* view was an older idea than the majority view: the majority was a means to an end, and the end was the *common*.

---

[36] *Constitutional History*, ii. 265.
[37] F. W. Maitland, *Township and Borough* (Cambridge, 1898), p. 35.
[38] Ibid., p. 34.
[39] Ibid., p. 32.

APPENDIX

Passages from the Rolls of the Parliaments (in translation)
illustrating certain points in Lectures 4 and 5.

A

Distinction between 'communes petitions' presented by the Commons
and 'singuleres petitions' presented by individual persons, particularly
as reflected in the different reception in parliament each sort was
accorded, i.e. the different channels they followed.

1346

And then it was asked of the knights, citizens and burgesses that if they
wished to submit any petition in the said parliament that might turn to
their common profit and easement, they should hand it in to the Clerk
of the Parliament: the which petition, delivered by them on the Friday
next following that Thursday, was considered in the presence of the
lords of the Council on Saturday, Sunday and Monday next following,
on which same Monday was an answer given to it.

(Rot. Parl. ii. 160 (11))

1348

And then the Commons were told that all individual persons (*singulers
persones*) who wished to hand in petitions in this parliament should
deliver them to the Chancellor; and that the petitions touching the
Commons they should deliver to the Clerk of the Parliament.

The which Commons delivered their petitions to the said Clerk in
the following manner. (*Rot. Parl.* ii. 201 (4))

1363

And so the parliament continued to treat of divers matters, touching as
well the petitions presented by the Commons and others, individual
persons, as the needs of the King and his kingdom, until Friday,
3 November, upon which day, the King, prelates, dukes, earls, barons
and Commons being in the White Chamber, and when the petitions
of the Commons and the answers made to them had been read, the
Chancellor, at the King's command, disclosed to the Lords and Commons that the King's will was to maintain and keep the ordinance made
about apparel. (*Rot. Parl.* ii. 280, no. 38)

1373

On which day [29 Nov.] the King, Prince, prelates, magnates and Commons being in the White Chamber, the Commons made a grant to the King, to help, sustain and maintain his wars against his enemies and also [assist] his subjects serving him overseas, a grant contained in a written, indentured schedule, unsealed, expressing the form and manner of it. This schedule they gave to the King, and it was there read, in his presence. . . . And then they gave in their petitions in writing, and prayed the King that these might be expedited and graciously answered. Which things the King cordially granted them.

And after this it was stated by the Chancellor that the King warmly thanked the Lords and Commons for the great aid with which they had supplied him; and it was the King's will that other, individual persons (*singulers persones*) who wanted to put forward their petitions should do so, delivering them to the Clerks designated for the purpose between then and Thursday following [1 Dec.], inclusive, when they would be answered in a proper manner. The names of the Clerks and also those of the Lords appointed to try and to determine them, have been written below. And it was told to the Commons that it pleased the King that those who wished to remain in order to wait for and receive answers to their petitions, and also to sue out their writs for expenses, might do so, the others departing at will. And so the parliament was dissolved. (*Rot. Parl.* ii.316(6), (7))

Jan. 1397

And then he [the Chancellor] said how the King had ordained and assigned certain Clerks to receive special petitions (*petitions especialx*) concerning causes and matters of interest to parliament, and certain Lords to try and to answer those same petitions in the customary manner, the names of which Clerks and Lords are as follows:- . . .

(*Rot. Parl.* iii.337 (2))

B

(i) *Definition of 'commune petition'*

1352

And now . . . the said Lord William [de Shareshull, C.J.K.B.] told the Commons that if they had any petitions concerning grievances done to common people, or to help improve the Law, they should put them forward in parliament. And it was also told to the Prelates and Lords that each should attend to the trying of the petitions of individual persons in the places appointed for them.

And then, following long discussion and deliberation by the Commons with the 'Communalte', and when the advice of some of the magnates had been conveyed to them both regarding an aid to be assigned to our Lord the King to withstand the malice of his adversary [of France] and with respect to the making of petitions touching the common people of the land, the said Commons came before our Lord the King and all the magnates in parliament and showed how the common people of the land were much impoverished as well by the deadly plague which had lately occurred there . . . as by other harsh taxes, tallages and many other adversities that had befallen them. But notwithstanding these mischiefs, and having regard to necessary measures of defence appropriate to the deliverance of the realm of England from the great malice of its enemies, they presented to our Lord the King in full parliament a roll containing the aid which they had ordained and, being of one accord, had unanimously granted to our Lord the King in his great necessity, and also the petitions touching the 'Commune' of the land, in respect of which they asked our Lord the King for a good and prompt response.   (*Rot. Parl.* ii.237(8) (9))

(ii) examples of 'common petitions'

(a)
1348 The Petitions of the Commons, and the replies to the same.

no. II   Item, the said 'Commune' prays that since, as is notoriously known throughout all the counties of England, robbers, thieves and other evildoers go on foot and ride on horseback in large bands throughout the land in divers places and commit larcenies and robberies, it may please our Lord the King to charge the magnates of the land not to maintain any such person, privily or openly; rather that they assist the arrest and capture of such ill-disposed people. That besides this there be now chosen, in this parliament, two magnates, the knights of each shire, and two men-of-law, who are to have a commission of *oyer and terminer* and promise parliament on oath loyally to enquire into and hear and determine such cases, at least three times a year; and that an established fee be provided for them out of the revenues accruing by virtue of their commissions. And that these same justices enquire about false money, and that the good money be in no way altered.
Answer: This was answered in the last parliament.

(*Rot. Parl.* ii.201(6))

(b)
Oct. 1377 Hereinafter follow the petitions put forward in Parliament by the Commons, with the answers thereto made and given them.

no. XXVIII Item, Forasmuch as men of religion purchase [or are donated] land and cause others to be enfeoffed of it, they themselves taking the profits, [it is requested] that in this event, and in all such other imaginable circumstances, they be adjudged liable under the statute *De religiosis*, and that the King and other lords have the benefit of the profits, as is ordained in the said statute.

Answer: The Lords are not minded to change the law as previously enforced. (*Rot. Parl.* iii.19(69))

C

Presentation of *singuleres petitions* 'in the name of the Commons', with special reference to the steps occasionally taken by the Commons to limit abuses of this practice.

Jan. 1327
[Following a number of petitions beginning 'The *Commune* prays our Lord the King and his Council', occurs this note:]

And should any other bill be put forward in the name of the *Commune*, we disavow it, except for this bill which takes the form of an indenture. (*Rot. Parl.* ii.10–11(38))

1348
Item, the *Commune* requests that the petitions delivered by the said *Commune* in the last parliament, and by our Lord the King, prelates and magnates of the land fully answered and granted, should hold good; and that the answers previously granted should not be changed by any bill delivered in this parliament in the name of the *Commune* or of anyone else. For if any such bill should be delivered in parliament in contravention, the *Commune* does not avow it.

Answer: On an earlier occasion the King, by advice of the prelates and magnates of the land, made answer to the petitions of the Commons touching the law of the land, [namely] that the laws established and in use in times past, and the legal procedure previously employed, could not be changed without a new statute being made on the subject. The King was unable to do this then and, for certain causes, has no intention of doing so now. However, as soon as he thinks it proper, he will consult with the magnates and the sages of his Council and, in respect of those articles and others touching amendment of the law, ordain by their advice and counsel in such a way that justice and equity be done to each and all of his lieges and subjects. (*Rot. Parl.* ii.203(30))

1372
The petitions which the Commons had put forward in parliament, and the answers given to them, were read. So also was an ordinance made in the same parliament, which is as follows. Forasmuch as lawyers, who prosecute divers business in the King's courts on behalf of individual persons by whom they are retained, procure and cause to be put forward in the name of the Commons a number of petitions which in no way

touch the Commons but touch only the individual persons by whom they are retained; and forasmuch, too, as sheriffs, who are officials serving the people generally and, in order to do justice to everyone, ought to be resident where they hold office, and yet who before now have been named and returned to parliament by themselves as knights of the shires; it was agreed and assented to in the parliament that no lawyer prosecuting business in the King's court or sheriff, when in office, be henceforward returned or accepted as knight of the shire, and that those who are lawyers and sheriffs and have now been returned to parliament are not to have their wages. Rather is it the King's will that knights and the worthiest serjeants of their countries be henceforward returned as knights of parliament, and that they be elected in full county court.   (*Rot. Parl.* ii.310(13))

1394

Item, the Commons request that all the good laws which have obtained in your [Richard II's] time and in the times of your very noble ancestors, be maintained and kept, without regard to any special plea. Now, in view of the fact that two chaplains, who claim to hold a chantry in the church of St. Mary Aldermary in London, have prosecuted a bill in the name of the Commons before our Lord the King and the Lords of this parliament in order, by a statute to be made in this present parliament, to give effect to divers testaments and bequests of tenements in London which use such words as, 'I leave two messuages etc. for the upkeep of two chaplains, or one chaplain, who will celebrate the divine office for my soul etc. in such and such a church' . . . , [the Commons request] that it may please your Highness to consider the damages which you and other landowners in similar case could incur, not to ordain any such statute as the said chaplains are prosecuting, especially with regard to any such bequest as has been made previously, until your very wise Council shall be fully aware of what damages you may incur, and not to change your very noble law made and hitherto used by you and your very noble ancestors.

Answer: Let the Common Law be used as previously.

(*Rot. Parl.* iii.321(44))

D

(i) Petitions adopted by the Commons, including petitions initially addressed to them, requesting, expressly or implicitly, their mediation.

1378

To the knights, citizens, burgesses and Commons of shires, the abbot and convent of Westminster make known that although they possess divers privileges and liberties, including one to the effect that if any fugitive comes within the precinct of their church he may, whatever the cause and whatever his rank, be safe there . . . and not legally charged by anybody (of which franchise they have been in peaceful possession from the time of St. Edward . . . without interruption), certain sons of iniquity did of late forcibly enter the said church and there, without any cause, killed Robert Hawley, a fugitive, and a servant of the church as well, and also arrested and abducted, alive, John Shakele, grievously molesting the monks and disturbing divine service there . . . , having no consideration for the dread censures applicable to all those who infringe the aforesaid privileges. [Wherefore] may it please you [the Commons] to help and advise the noble Lords of the parliament so that it may please them to ordain appropriate remedy and due restitution to the said church, for the salvation of the privileges and liberties granted by the noble kings, Edgar, St. Edward and other kings their successors, the lords and commons of the realm, so that divine services may be celebrated appropriately, to the honour of God, of St. Peter and St. Edward, and of the Relics which have their resting place there, and also for the souls of their own noble ancestors.

Be it recorded that this bill was delivered on behalf of our Lord the King to the Clerk of the Parliament, so that it might be put into the files, etc., the which bill was, in the name of the Commons attending this parliament, presented to our Lord the King and his Council for their consideration.   (*Rot. Parl.* iii.50 (no. 3))

1393
Petition of the Commons to the King

Item, the Commons show how, because of the prisage of wines entering the kingdom, the merchants who pay prise are greatly oppressed, damaged and undone, but with little profit or advantage to our said Lord the King: wherefore, the aforesaid merchants, for the greater profit and advantage of our Lord the King, and for their own relief, do supplicate your Highness that they may be acquitted of such prises, paying for each tun of wine subject to prise 20*d.* and for each pipe of wine 10*d.*, as do aliens, at the ports where they unload them. Saving always to all cities, boroughs and lords, their liberties and franchises. Answer: If they will pay 2*s.* for each tun of wine throughout the kingdom, both within franchises and outside, the King wills that they be quit of his prise. And if not, let the practice be as heretofore.
                                      (*Rot. Parl.* iii.306–7(29))

1402
Our very dread and excellent Lord the King, your humble lieges, the Commons of your realm now assembled, do petition that, in order to relieve your counties of Northumberland, Cumberland, and Newcastle-on-Tyne of the losses and damages they have now lately suffered

because of Scotland . . . , by reason of which a thousand people and more have left those parts, it may please your Royal Majesty to pardon your said three counties, and now release and discharge their people from, all manner of [penalties for] escapes of felons, fines, issues and amercements, all manner of tenths, fifteenths, debts, prests and accounts, together with arrears tried and not determined, and that they may receive allowances in your Exchequer; so that by this grace and pardon your said subjects may have a better will to return to their countries, to recover their lands and inheritances, and be more inclined to support their obligations and, in future, defend their Marches. For God and as a work of charity.

Answer: The King has granted this petition according to the purport thereof.   (Rot. Parl. iii.518(17))

1402

To the very wise Commons of this present parliament humbly petition John Hall and Katherine his wife that. . .

Answer: Let it be committed to the Council, to act toward the parties, touching the substance of the petition, by authority of parliament.
                                                       (Rot. Parl. iii.512(no. 3))

1410

For Sir Walter Hungerford   Item, the same day [Friday 2nd May], a petition was put forward by the Commons in parliament for Sir Walter Hungerford, in the following form—May it please the very wise Commons of this present parliament to know that it has been found by an inquest procured before certain commissioners, appointed in the county of Wiltshire by letters patent of our Lord the King, that Walter Hungerford, knight, did cause divers wastes, destruction and dilapidations in the [alien] priory of Farleigh, and in the lands and tenements belonging to the said priory, when, as was recently the case, he and William Stourton had the custody of the priory with appurtenances by our Lord the King's letters patent, which . . . presentment he proposes to traverse, as he well and clearly can do. Wherefore may it please the said wise Commons to make a special request to our said Lord the King, that it be ordained by authority of this parliament that the sheriff of the said county shall not, in the inquest to be made on the said traverse, return the name of any man [as a juror] who has not at least £20 worth of land in the same county, and this on pain of £200 to be paid to our said Lord the King. And if the sheriff return otherwise, that the return so made be null and void.

Answer: Which petition, read and understood, was answered in the following words: *Le roy le voet.*   (Rot. Parl. iii.632(40))

1421

To the worthy, wise, and discrete persons [the] Speker of this present

Parlement and . . . alle the Knyghtes of the Shires. Prayen and requiren
. . . the pore liege men and Soudeors in the town of Caleys, that hit like
to yours wise and gode discrecions tenderly to considere, how that the
pore Soudeors be the space of V yeer a quarter except . . . hav truly
served the sauf garde of the forsaid town withoute . . . plein paiement
. . . . Wherefore, like unto youre high discrecions to have recomaunded,
amonge alle youre other peticions, the forseid town. And *for to be gode
menes* to . . . the King . . . *youre gode and graciouse mediacion* so to be
preferred . . . (editor's italics). (*Rot. Parl.* iv.159(no. 5))

1423
Common Petitions presented by the Commons

Against John, Lord Talbot, and other evildoers — Item, the Commons request that, because divers lieges of our . . . Lord the King have piteously and grievously shown, by their divers bills presented to the said Commons in this present parliament, that many and divers extortions, oppressions, murders, homicides, forcible and wrongful ejections from lands and tenements etc. have been discovered in the hundred of Wormelow in Herefordshire . . . , it may please . . . the duke of Gloucester . . . and the Lords Spiritual and Temporal in this parliament to make Lord Talbot and other evildoers of his party . . . find individually . . . sufficient surety for keeping the peace towards the king's lieges . . .

(*Rot. Parl.* iv.254(46))

(ii) Petitions adopted by the Commons on behalf of individual persons,
recognized as a separate category of petitions.

1425
It was ordained and agreed to in this present parliament by the advice
of the Lords Spiritual and Temporal, and with the assent of the Commons in this parliament, that all the petitions presented in the same
parliament by the Commons for particular and private persons (*pur
especialx et privatz persones*) and not answered, should be committed to
the King's Council by the above-mentioned authority [the authority
of parliament] to hear all the matters comprised in those petitions and,
according to their discretion, good faith and conscience, to determine
them. (*Rot. Parl.* iv.301(21))

INDEX